D0862674

Lutheranism 101
THE COURSE

Written by
Shawn L. Kumm

General Editor
Scot A. Kinnaman

CONCORDIA PUBLISHING HOUSE · SAINT LOUIS

Copyright © 2011 Concordia Publishing House
3558 S. Jefferson Ave., St. Louis, MO 63118-3968
1-800-325-3040 • www.cph.org

All rights reserved. No part of this publication may be reproduced, stored in a retrieval system, or transmitted, in any form or by any means, electronic, mechanical, photocopying, recording, or otherwise, without the prior written permission of Concordia Publishing House.

Scripture quotations are from the ESV Bible® (The Holy Bible, English Standard Version®), copyright © 2001 by Crossway Bibles, a publishing ministry of Good News Publishers. Used by permission. All rights reserved.

Quotations from the Lutheran Confessions are from Concordia: The Lutheran Confessions, second edition; edited by Paul McCain, et al., copyright © 2006 Concordia Publishing House. All rights reserved.

Quotations with the abbreviation LSB are from Lutheran Service Book, copyright © 2006 Concordia Publishing House. All rights reserved.

The quotations from the Small Catechism are from Luther's Small Catechism with Explanation, copyright © 1986, 1991 Concordia Publishing House. All rights reserved.

Manufactured in the United States of America

1 2 3 4 5 6 7 8 9 10   20 19 18 17 16 15 14 13 12 11

Contents

Part Five: Worship: The Blessings of God

Part Six: Living as Lutherans

A Pastor's Daily Prayer

Introduction

What Is This Book?

Lutheranism 101: The Course works closely with *Lutheranism 101* to take the reader deeper into the teaching, doctrine, or practice being presented. Sometimes that means digging into the text of *Lutheranism 101* and exploring connections that are being made. Other times it means working with Scripture or some of the primary Lutheran resources for doctrine and practice. For those new to Lutheranism and for those who want a fresh approach to the heritage of what Lutherans believe, teach, and confess, *Lutheranism 101* together with *Lutheranism 101: The Course* helps create a solid foundation upon which a lifetime of sound teaching can be built.

Besides your personal copy of *Lutheranism 101*, it will be useful to have these books with you as you work through *The Course*:

- **Bible.** While any good translation will work, comments and quotations in *Lutheranism 101* and *The Course* are based upon the English Standard Version (ESV). When choosing a Bible, we suggest that it is best to use a translation instead of a paraphrase. A paraphrase offers a phrase-by-phrase restatement of a biblical text, giving you the general meaning. A paraphrase is often simpler to read, but may not faithfully represent what the biblical authors wrote. A translation works carefully with each word in the original language (Hebrew, Aramaic, or Greek) in a way that captures the precise meaning and personal style of the original biblical writer. Some translations are very literal and present a near word-for-word correspondence with the original text. The best translations will take into account differences in grammar, syntax, and expression between the English and the original language, to offer the reader not only a Bible that is true to the original but also a Bible that is understandable and reads well. A study Bible includes added notes and resources that help explain the Bible.

- **Book of Concord.** The Book of Concord is a collection of statements of faith written by Lutheran Christians in the sixteenth century when they were risking their lives to stand up for the Bible being the basis for belief and practice in the Church. It was first published in 1580. There are several great translations of the 1580 Book of Concord from which to choose, but we have cited *Concordia: The Lutheran Confessions*, 2nd ed. (St. Louis: Concordia, 2006).

- **Hymnal.** Hymnals offer excellent resources for individual worship and prayer in addition to settings for worship (Divine Service) and hymns. Having a hymnal at home will enrich your Sunday worship experience by giving you and your family the opportunity to become more familiar with the contents of the hymnal when you have more time and fewer distractions than we commonly have at church on Sundays. Throughout *The Course* you will be directed to *Lutheran Service Book*, which is the hymnal used by much of The Lutheran Church—Missouri Synod.

- **Small Catechism.** Martin Luther wrote his Small Catechism almost 500 years ago as a resource to help parents and pastors teach the basics of faith. While the Small Catechism is included in the Book of Concord and in many contemporary Lutheran hymnals, recent English editions include extra explanations that make the catechism even more helpful as a teaching and learning tool.

How Do I Use This Book?

The Course can be used by groups, families, and individuals who want to dig deeper into what it means to be Lutheran. After reading a chapter in *Lutheranism 101*, turn to the corresponding chapter in *The Course* and work through the questions. A leader's guide is available as a free download. The leader's guide will give you even more information, whether you are working as part of a group or individually.

To download the leader's guide, go to **lutheranism101.com** and click on "The Course" at the top of the page.

Abbreviations

You will see many quotations from the Lutheran Confessions as found in the Book of Concord. The following lists provides abbreviations used, what they mean, and examples of how you would find the text.

AC   Augsburg Confession
Ap   Apology of the Augsburg Confession
Ep   Epitome of the Formula of Concord
FC   Formula of Concord
LC   Large Catechism
SA   Smalcald Articles
SC   Small Catechism
SD   Solid Declaration of the Formula of Concord
Tr   Treatise on the Power and Primacy of the Pope

EXAMPLES:
AC XX 4 (Augsburg Confession, Article XX, paragraph 4)
Ap IV 229 (Apology of the AC, Article IV, paragraph 229)
FC SD X 24 (Solid Declaration of the Formula of Concord, Article X, paragraph 24)
FC Ep V 8 (Epitome of the Formula of Concord, Article V, paragraph 8)
LC V 32, 37 (Large Catechism, Part 5, paragraphs 32 and 37)
SA III I 6 (Smalcald Articles, Part III, Article I, paragraph 6)
SC III 5 (Small Catechism, Part III, paragraph 5)

Prayers

Some prayers end with a number in parentheses. This number indicates the source of the prayer in the various products of *Lutheran Service Book*. All collects, prayers, intercessions, thanksgivings, and prayers in the service orders, *Altar Book*, or *Agenda* of *Lutheran Service Book* copyright © 2006 Concordia Publishing House. Prayers taken from *Lutheran Service Book: Pastoral Care Companion* copyright © 2007 Concordia Publishing House.

PART ONE

It's All about the Relationships

What you'll learn about:

- God reveals Himself in three persons: Father, Son, and Holy Spirit.

- God has a fundamental problem with us called sin, and this problem has deadly consequences.

- While we cannot solve the problem of sin, God's plan of salvation redeems us from the consequences of sin and brings us into a relationship with Him.

- Only faith in Jesus Christ saves us.

- On the Last Day, Jesus will return and pass eternal judgment on all believers and unbelievers; the believers will begin to enjoy everlasting life with God, while unbelievers will be forever separated from God.

CHAPTER 1

Who Is God? pp. 26–30

BELIEVE, TEACH, CONFESS

The Father, Son, and Holy Spirit, three distinct persons in one divine essence and nature [Matthew 28:19], are one God, who has created heaven and earth [1 Corinthians 8:6].

The Father is begotten of no one; the Son is begotten of the Father [John 1:14]; the Holy Spirit proceeds from the Father and the Son [John 15:26].

Neither the Father nor the Holy Spirit, but the Son became man [John 1:14].

The Son became man in this manner: He was conceived, without the cooperation of man, by the Holy Spirit [Luke 1:34–35], and was born of the pure, holy Virgin Mary. Afterward, He suffered, died, was buried, descended to hell, rose from the dead [1 Corinthians 15:3–4], ascended to heaven [Acts 1:9–11], sits at the right hand of God [Acts 2:33], will come to judge the quick and the dead, and so on, as the Apostles' and Athanasian Creeds and our children's catechism teach. (SA I 1–4)

Key Bible Verse:

Your righteousness, O God,
   reaches the high heavens.
You who have done great things,
   O God, who is like you? (Psalm 71:19)

Review

1. What are three ways we know God exists?

_____

_____

_____

2. Turn to the Athanasian Creed in your hymnal (if you have *Lutheran Service Book*, it's on pages 319–320). Read through the creed and note verses that are helpful for you in this statement of the Holy Trinity. Also note those verses that may be troubling.

Connect

3. Read the second "From the Bible" box on p. 30. The statement is made that "it is the existence of goodness and beauty and love that is most remarkable." How does Joseph understand this statement in Genesis 50:15–21 and St. Paul in Romans 8:28?

Ponder

4. Write down three examples of false gods. What characteristics assigned to these false gods shows these gods to have been invented by man and fashioned in man's image?

_____

_____

_____

_____

_____

_____

5. Consider this statement: "The Triune God is not a god someone would think up." What biblical evidence in Chapter 1 supports this? Also study the following Scripture passages: Psalm 139:13–14; 1 Corinthians 8:1–6; Hebrews 3:1–6; 1 Kings 18:20–29.

6. How is what you have learned about God—Father, Son, and Holy Spirit—a comfort to you in your daily life?

Pray

O Holy Trinity, Father, Son and Spirit, to You I give all honor, glory, and praise for Your love shown in creating me, in saving me, and in keeping me in the one true faith. In Your triune name I pray. Amen.

HYMN

O blessèd, holy Trinity,
Divine, eternal Unity,
O Father, Son, and Holy Ghost,
This day Your name be uppermost.
Lord, bless and keep me as Your
   own;
Lord, look in kindness from Your
   throne;
Lord, shine unfailing peace on me
By grace surrounded; set me free.
—"O Blessed, Holy Trinity"
   (*LSB* 876:1, 4)

CHAPTER 2

That's a Sin pp. 31–35

Key Bible Verse

As for me, I said, "O Lord, be gracious to me;
heal me, for I have sinned against You!" (Psalm 41:4)

Review

1. The built-in order of God's creation also includes the built-in order of His moral law. Read page 31. What are some ways people try to explain away sin?

2. Two important distinctions are made concerning sin. There is original sin and there is actual sin. Reread page 32, the call-out box on page 33, and then pages 33–34. Write down a definition of original sin. Read pp. 32–33 and write down a definition of actual sin.

3. Read Psalm 7:14 and James 1:12–15. Discuss how these verses describe both original sin and actual sin.

BELIEVE, TEACH, CONFESS

The knowledge of original sin is absolutely necessary. The magnitude of Christ's grace cannot be understood unless our diseases are recognized. ‹Christ says in Matthew 9:12 and Mark 2:17, "Those who are well have no need of a physician."› The entire notion that a person is righteous is mere hypocrisy before God. We must acknowledge that our heart is, by nature, destitute of fear, love, and confidence in God. For this reason the prophet Jeremiah says, "After I was instructed, I slapped my thigh; I was ashamed, and I was confounded" (31:19). Likewise, "I said in my alarm, 'All mankind are liars' " (Psalm 116:11). That is, they do not think correctly about God. (Ap II 33–34)

Connect

4. God deals with sin in two ways. The first way is with the Law, which convicts us of our sin. The second way is with the Gospel, which forgives us our sin. Read the following Scripture passages and determine which is used—the Law, the Gospel, or both: Jeremiah 33:8; Ezekiel 18:30; Hosea 6:1. See Chapter 16 if you need help with distinguishing Law and Gospel.

Ponder

5. Consider the following statements in light of the Ten Commandments: "I really didn't say much about her affair. God knows I could have said more. Their marriage isn't going to last anyway. The kids will be okay. Anyway, I knew you would want to hear this; this job is so boring and we need a bit of livening up today." Explain how each of the Commandments is broken in this example.

> **HYMN**
>
> I lay my sins on Jesus,
> The spotless Lamb of God;
> He bears them all and frees us
> From the accursed load.
> I bring my guilt to Jesus
> To wash my crimson stains
> Clean in His blood most precious
> Till not a spot remains.
> —"I Lay My Sins on Jesus"
> (*LSB* 606:1)

Pray

O Lord Jesus, by sinful birth I have complete and utter disregard for Your Holy Word. Through Your cleansing and life-giving Word I now have hope and eternal life. As I continue to struggle with sin, give me the aid of Your Spirit that I may not fall into any kind of sin but obey Your holy ways. In Your name, O Christ, I pray. Amen.

CHAPTER 3

It's All about Jesus
Part 1 pp. 36–42

BELIEVE, TEACH, CONFESS

We believe, teach, and confess that now, in this one undivided person of Christ, there are two distinct natures: the divine, which is from eternity, and the human, which in time was received into the unity of the person of God's Son. These two natures in the person of Christ are never either separated from or mingled with each other. Nor are they changed into each other. Each one abides in its nature and essence in the person of Christ to all eternity. (FC SD VIII 7)

Key Bible Verse

Therefore God has highly exalted Him and bestowed on Him the name that is above every name, so that at the name of Jesus every knee should bow, in heaven and on earth and under the earth, and every tongue confess that Jesus Christ is Lord, to the glory of God the Father. (Philippians 2:9–11)

Review

1. Summarize the two pillars that teach us about Jesus.

2. What are some benefits to confessing the Creeds weekly and regularly?

Connect

3. Someone says to you, "Jesus was a nice guy, and not a bad teacher either. But the eternal Son of God? Ha!" What scriptural evidence could you present to this person to show Jesus really is the Son of God? Here are three for starters: Matthew 16:13–20; Matthew 27:54; 1 John 1:1–3; 5:20. The two pages of biblical names and titles of Jesus at the end of this chapter might also be useful (pp. 41–42).

4. Spend some time looking for the Old Testament counterparts to the New Testament names given to Jesus on pages 41–42. For example: Good Shepherd (John 10:11, 14) finds its Old Testament foreshadowing in Psalm 23, and "Bread of life" (John 6:35, 48) in Exodus 16:13–15. The margin notes of a good study Bible should help locate the Old Testament verses. At what times in your life are these names of Jesus a comfort to you?

a.

b.

c.

Ponder

5. In Chapter 3 this statement is made, "Take Jesus out of the message of the Church or out of a person's faith and it is no longer Christian!" (p. 36). Write down two messages, either from bumper stickers, wall hangings, or billboards that sound Christian but really aren't, or are incomplete in their definition and meaning. Discuss how these sayings fall short. For example: "Believe!" Believe in what? Believe in whom? Why believe? How will such belief come about?

a.

b.

6. Hebrews 4:15 is quoted on page 39. There we learn that Jesus is "one who in every respect has been tempted as we are, yet without sin." What relief do you find in knowing that you have a Savior who knows *exactly* how you feel when tempted? Are there any temptations Jesus experienced that surprise you? See Hebrews 2:14–18 for further comfort.

Pray

Lord Jesus, may my knee bow and my tongue confess You to be Lord. I praise You for Your divine work in conquering my enemies. Help me to remember You are with me when I am tempted. Turn this to holy testing and show me the way out so I do not sin. All glory to Your Father for sending You to all humanity—and to me. Amen.

> **HYMN**
>
> Jesus! Name of
>   wondrous love,
> Name all other names above,
> Unto which must ev'ry knee
> Bow in deep humility.
> Jesus! Name of priceless worth
> To the fallen of the earth
> For the promise that it gave,
> "Jesus shall His people save."
> —"Jesus! Name of Wondrous Love"
>   (*LSB* 900:1, 3)

CHAPTER 4

It's All about Jesus
Part 2 pp. 43–44

BELIEVE, TEACH, CONFESS

We believe, teach, and confess that according to the usage of Holy Scripture the word justify means, in this article, "to absolve, that is, to declare free from sins." Proverbs 17:15 says, "He who justifies the wicked and he who condemns the righteous are both alike an abomination to the Lord." *Also Romans 8:33 says, "Who shall bring any charge against God's elect? It is God who justifies." (FC Ep III 7)*

Key Bible Verse:

[Jesus said,] "I tell you, this man went down to his house justified . . . ." (Luke 18:14)

Review

1. Today's computers make justified margins instantaneous. The left margin on this page is "justified." It is straight and true. The margin on the right of this page is ragged and uneven. Imagine, then, the cross of Christ being pushed up against this right margin, bringing it into perfect alignment with God. This is what Christ's cross does to you. Jesus takes what is sinful and out-of-sync with God's holiness and purity, and He makes your life holy, straight and true with His Father. Read Isaiah 45:17, 25; and 1 Corinthians 6:9–11. According to these passages discuss how God's justifying work is accomplished for you, through, and by, Christ.

2. "Justification is not by what we do or who we are" (p. 44). In what ways does our sinful flesh try to make justification about something we do or about who we are? For examples, see Matthew 19:16–22 and John 8:31–38.

Connect

3. The doctrine of justification ("we are justified by grace through faith in Jesus Christ"–p. 43) is called the teaching upon which the Church stands or falls. Why do all other teachings from Scripture flow from the doctrine of justification? What is at risk if the focus is elsewhere? How would this cause the Church to fall?

Ponder

4. Read Luke 18:9–14, the parable of the Pharisee and the tax collector. A key point to understanding this parable is to remember *who* is telling the parable. To whom does Jesus speak this parable? Who speaks justification upon the tax collector? The temple was the place of sacrifice. Matthew tells us what happens in the temple when Jesus was sacrificed on the cross (Matthew 27:51). How can Jesus declare you justified?

Prayer

Dearest Jesus, because of Your great love for mankind, and also for me, You have made right what was wrong, You have made what once was crooked now straight. For justifying me before God through Your death upon the cross, I give You the deepest thanks, O Christ my Lord. Amen.

HYMN

Look unto Him, ye nations;
 own Your God, ye fallen race.
Look and be saved through faith alone,
Be justified by grace.
See all your sins on Jesus laid;
The Lamb of God was slain.
His soul was once an off'ring made
For ev'ry soul of man.
—"Oh, for a Thousand Tongues to Sing" (*LSB* 528:5–6)

Putting It All Together:
Getting Right with God pp. 45–50

Looking it up

1. Scripture speaks of Jesus as our "scapegoat" (p. 47). Read Leviticus 16:1–19. Note three major things about the goat that is sacrificed.

    a.

    b.

    c.

2. What was the problem with Old Testament sacrifices? Read Hebrews 10:1–14. Where and why do the sacrifices finally end?

Linking it up

The Augsburg Confession, which begins the formal statements in the Book of Concord, is the Lutheran understanding of Scripture. Succinct and to the point, this confession was presented before the Holy Roman Emperor Charles V on June 25, 1530.

Article 1 of the Augsburg Confession (AC I 2–3) affirms the biblical teaching of who God is (One God in three persons) and that He is "of infinite . . . goodness" (see also Chapter 1, p. 29). After establishing the goodness and therefore the holiness of God, **Article II** gets to the heart of the problem—sin, our sin.

> Our churches teach that since the fall of Adam [Romans 5:12], all who are naturally born are born with sin [Psalm 51:5], that is, without the fear of God, without trust in God, and with the inclination to sin, called concupiscence. Concupiscence is a disease and original vice that is truly sin. It damns and brings eternal death on those who are not born anew through Baptism and the Holy Spirit [John 3:5]. (AC II 1–2)

In contrast to God, who is holy, our sin stands in stark and dark contrast. The question is then this: who will save us? This question is answered in **Article III** of the Confession:

> Our churches teach that the Word, that is, the Son of God [John 1:14], assumed the human nature in the womb of the Blessed Virgin Mary. So there are two natures—the divine and the human—inseparably joined in one person. There is one Christ, true God and true man, who was born of the Virgin Mary, truly suffered, was crucified, died, and was buried. He did this to reconcile the Father to us and to be a sacrifice, not only for original guilt, but also for all actual sins of mankind [John 1:29]. (AC III 1–3)

How then does this Good News that Jesus is the full and final sacrifice for our sins become ours? This is answered in **Article IV** of the Augsburg Confession:

Our churches teach that people cannot be justified before God by their own strength, merits, or works. People are freely justified for Christ's sake, through faith, when they believe that they are received into favor and that their sins are forgiven for Christ's sake. By His death, Christ made satisfaction for our sins. God counts this faith for righteousness in His sight [Romans 3:21–26; 4:5]. (AC IV 1–3).

This is the most wonderful news we will ever hear. Yes, how will people hear this good news? **Article V** has this to say,

So that we may obtain this faith, the ministry of teaching the Gospel and administering the Sacraments was instituted. Through the Word and Sacraments, as through instruments, the Holy Spirit is given [John 20:22]. He works faith, when and where it pleases God [John 3:8], in those who hear the good news that God justifies those who believe that they are received into grace for Christ's sake. This happens not through our own merits, but for Christ's sake. (AC V 1–3)

This article is also expanded in Chapter 12, "God's Deliverymen."

3. Outline the five main points made in the articles of the Augsburg Confession stated above, using only one word for each point.

    a. Article I:

    b. Article II:

    c. Article III:

    d. Article IV:

    e. Article V:

4. What ways could these five points be used to share with others the work of Jesus?

Lifting it up

Lord Jesus Christ, our great High Priest, cleanse us by the power of Your redeeming blood that in purity and peace we may worship and adore Your holy name; for You live and reign with the Father and the Holy Spirit, one God, now and forever. Amen. (B84)

HYMN

Not all the blood of beasts
On Jewish altars slain
Could give the guilty conscience peace
Or wash away the stain.
But Christ, the heav'nly Lamb,
Takes all our sins away;
A sacrifice of nobler name
And richer blood than they.
—"Not All the Blood of Beasts"
(*LSB* 431:1–2)

CHAPTER 5

It's the End of the World as We Know It

pp. 51–58

Believe, Teach, Confess

For the coming of God's kingdom to us happens in two ways: (a) here in time through the Word and faith [Matthew 13]; and (b) in eternity forever through revelation [Luke 19:11; 1 Peter 1:4–5]. Now we pray for both these things. We pray that the kingdom may come to those who are not yet in it, and, by daily growth that it may come to us who have received it, both now and hereafter in eternal life. All this is nothing other than saying, "Dear Father, we pray, give us first Your Word, so that the Gospel may be preached properly throughout the world. Second, may the Gospel be received in faith and work and live in us, so that through the Word and the Holy Spirit's power [Romans 15:18–19], Your kingdom may triumph among us. And we pray that the devil's kingdom be put down [Luke 11:17–20], so that he may have no right or power over us [Luke 10:17–19; Colossians 1], until at last his power may be utterly destroyed. So sin, death, and hell shall be exterminated [Revelation 20:13–14]. Then we may live forever in perfect righteousness and blessedness" [Ephesians 4:12–13]. (LC III 53–54)

Key Bible Verse

But the LORD sits enthroned forever;
He has established His throne for justice,
and He judges the world with righteousness;
He judges the peoples with uprightness. (Psalm 9:7–8)

Review

1. Lutheran theology strives for accuracy and detail. Points, sub-points, and sub-sub-points are used. We make no apologies for details when it comes to the Word of God. And so when we pray in the Second Petition of the Lord's Prayer, "Thy kingdom come," there is more to this than just a simple "kingdom." *Luther's Small Catechism with Explanation*, Question 212, teaches us that there are three kingdoms.

   The kingdom of power (God rules over all things and all people)

   The kingdom of grace (God rules over His Church on earth with His forgiving gifts)

   The kingdom of glory (God rules over the saints and angels of heaven)

The hymnal and prayer book of the Old Testament—the Psalms—have much to say about these three kingdoms. Read the following passages and decide whether the Scripture text describes the kingdom of power, the kingdom of grace, or the kingdom of glory.

Psalm 148:13 _____

Psalm 67:1–2 _____

Psalm 62:11 _____

Psalm 68:28 _____

Psalm 86:5–6 _____

Psalm 135:6 _____

Psalm 29:13 _____

Psalm 33:4–5 _____

Connect

2. What does Jesus mean in John 18:33–37 when He says, "My kingdom is not of this world?"

Ponder

3. If Jesus is to reign on earth for a literal 1,000 years (and He is not), what do you think year 999 would be like? One of sorrow? Joy? Panic? Review page 52. Read the following Scripture passages for the unbound and timeless promises of God to you.

Matthew 28:20b

Hebrews 13:8

Haggai 1:13

Genesis 28:15

4. Jesus never asks us to do something He hasn't done first. What comfort is yours knowing Jesus waits *with* you for the end of all things? How does this knowledge affect what you see in the tabloids and hear from hyper-televangelists who try to frighten their audience?

5. On page 53 the point is made that the end of the world isn't about *when* but about *how* you will be judged. So, how will you be judged? See page 54 for help, and read 2 Timothy 4:8 and John 5:19–24 for reassurance and hope.

2 Timothy 4:8

John 5:19–24

Pray

O Lord of all time and all knowledge, comfort me with the joy of Your return that I may be prepared to see You face-to-face and to enjoy everlasting peace because of Your cross-given gifts to me. In Jesus' name. Amen.

> **HYMN**
>
> The day is surely drawing near
> When Jesus, God's anointed,
> In all His power shall appear
> As judge whom God appointed.
> Then fright shall banish idle mirth,
> And flames on flames shall ravage earth
> As Scripture long has warned us.
> The final trumpet then shall sound
> And all the earth be shaken,
> And all who rest beneath the ground
> Shall from their sleep awaken.
> But all who live will in that hour,
> By God's almighty, boundless pow'r,
> Be changed at His commanding.
> —"The Day Is Surely Drawing Near" (*LSB* 508:1–2)

CHAPTER 6

The Last Stop pp. 59–62

Key Bible Verses

"O death, where is your victory? O death, where is your sting?" The sting of death is sin, and the power of sin is the law. But thanks be to God, who gives us the victory through our Lord Jesus Christ. (1 Corinthians 15:55–57)

Review

1. Study the key Bible verses above. Death is a Law topic. Which parts of the verses above are Law? Which parts are Gospel? Why is it important to know the difference? (For a review of Law and Gospel, see Chapter 16.)

2. Again, we continue to hone our skills distinguishing Law and Gospel. An essential Scripture passage to the discussion of death is Romans 6:23, "For the wages of sin is death, but the free gift of God is eternal life in Christ Jesus our Lord." Which part of the verse is Law? Which part is Gospel? How does the Gospel outweigh the Law? Why is this important?

BELIEVE, TEACH, CONFESS

But deliver us from evil.
What does this mean?
Answer: We pray in this petition, as in a summary, that our Father in heaven would deliver us from all kinds of evil, of body and soul, property and honor. And finally, when our last hour shall come, we pray that He would grant us a blessed end and graciously take us from this vale of tears to Himself into heaven. Amen. (SC III Seventh Petition)

Connect

3. Read Acts 26:28. If you have time, read Acts 25–26 for the entire account. Whether we have a short amount of time or long, what is necessary to convince someone Jesus is the Savior of the world, the only answer for death and the only giver of heaven?

Ponder

4. Read Isaiah 25:8 and Revelation 7:17; 21:4. From what tearful events and memories do you look forward to God wiping away all of your sadness?

5. How do you imagine heaven? Is it all fun and games, or something far more than that? For the connection between Christ's conquering death and resurrection and the heavenly banquet, read Isaiah 25:6–9 and Revelation 19:6–10.

Pray

O Lord, who has conquered death and the grave, even as I await my own death, keep me steadfast in the true faith. Focus my eyes solely on Your cross and Your own empty grave that I may be comforted when my eyes close in death. Jesus, in Your risen and victorious name I pray. Amen.

HYMN

Lord, it belongs not
   to my care
Whether I die or live;
To love and serve Thee is my share,
And this Thy grace must give.
If life be long, I will be glad
That I may long obey;
If short, yet why should I be sad
To soar to endless day?
—"Lord, It Belongs Not to My Care"
   (*LSB* 757:1–2)

Putting It All Together:
The Certainty of Faith pp. 63–66

Looking it up

1. Read John 20. What convinces Mary Magdalene and the ten disciples that Jesus was raised from the dead? In his doubt, did Thomas have the freedom to choose salvation? See also "Free to Choose" on pp. 65–66.

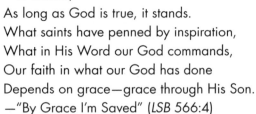

HYMN

By grace! This ground of faith
    is certain;
As long as God is true, it stands.
What saints have penned by inspiration,
What in His Word our God commands,
Our faith in what our God has done
Depends on grace—grace through His Son.
—"By Grace I'm Saved" (LSB 566:4)

Lifting it up

Almighty and ever-living God, You strengthened Your apostle Thomas with firm and certain faith in the resurrection of Your Son. Grant us such faith in Jesus Christ, our Lord and our God, that we may never be found wanting in Your sight; through the same Jesus Christ, who lives and reigns with You and the Holy Spirit, one God, now and forever. Amen. (F02)

Linking it up

2. After the Augsburg Confession was presented, Roman Catholic theologians responded in kind. The *Pontifical Confutation of the Augsburg Confession* was publicly read for the Lutherans, but they were not provided with a copy. Working from a carefully taken set of stenographer's notes, Philip Melanchthon began work on a faithful, scriptural explanation and response. This document is known as the *Apology* [or Defense] *of the Augsburg Confession*. Melanchthon completed the document on April 15, 1531.

> Therefore, by faith alone we receive forgiveness of sins when we comfort our hearts with confidence in the mercy promised for Christ's sake. Likewise, Paul says in Romans 5:2, "Through Him we have also obtained access" and adds, "by faith." Therefore, we are reconciled to the Father and receive forgiveness of sins when we are comforted with confidence in the mercy promised for Christ's sake. The adversaries regard Christ as Mediator and Atoning Sacrifice for this reason: He has merited the habit of love. They do not encourage us to use Him now as Mediator. They act as though Christ were certainly in the grave. They imagine that we have access to God through our own works. They think they merit this habit through these, and afterward, by this love, come to God. Is this not to bury Christ altogether and to take away the entire teaching of faith? Paul, on the contrary, teaches that we have access to God (that is, reconciliation) through Christ. To show how this happens, he adds that we have access by faith. By faith, for Christ's sake, we receive forgiveness of sins. (Ap IV 80–81)

Summarize in two parts the case of the Lutherans and that of the Roman Catholics.

Delivering the Gifts of God

What you'll learn about:

- God reveals Himself through human reason and through Scripture.

- Lutherans embrace the paradoxes of Scripture.

- The Church is a community of believers who are united in faith in Jesus Christ and has members in both heaven and on earth.

- The Church can be recognized through the marks of the Church.

- The Lutheran Church honors the saints as examples of faith and holy living.

- The government exercises the sword of God's power to establish order and peace.

- The Church's authority is the Office of the Keys, administered by her pastors.

- Christians are divided by not agreeing on what God's Word teaches.

- While all people have equal status in the Church, there are different roles.

CHAPTER 7

The Conundrum of Faith
pp. 70–72

BELIEVE, TEACH, CONFESS

Concerning our Lord and Savior Jesus Christ, as our only Teacher, this solemn command has been given from heaven to all people, "listen to Him" [Matthew 17:5]. He is not a mere man or angel, neither is He just true, wise, and mighty, but He is the eternal Truth and Wisdom itself and Almighty God. He knows very well what and how He is to speak. He can also powerfully effect and do everything that He says and promises. He says, "Heaven and earth will pass away, but My words will not pass away" (Luke 21:33); "All authority in heaven and on earth has been given to Me" (Matthew 28:18). (FC SD VII 43)

Key Bible Verse

Every word of God proves true;
He is a shield to those who take refuge
in Him. (Proverbs 30:5)

Review

1. During the High Middle Ages theology was known as "the Queen of Sciences." So highly regarded was theology at major European universities that theology professors led the academic processions. This is no longer so; that distinction is now caught in a tug-of-war somewhere between mathematics and physics. Compare Ecclesiastes 1:12–18; John 20:30–31; and 21:25. Where does the Christ-centered study of God's Word find itself in the present world of intellectual thought?

2. What winsome arguments do you need in order to have a discussion with unbelievers about the truth and importance of God's Word? How would the following verses stand up in today's academic world? Read Hebrews 11:1–3; 2 Peter 3:5; and Isaiah 40:6–8.

Connect

3. Marathon runners describe a phenomenon known as "hitting the wall," usually around the twentieth mile. Turn to the Athanasian Creed in *Lutheran Service Book,* p. 319. If possible, read the creed responsively whole verse by whole verse. At what point do you "hit the wall" when contemplating the inner workings of the Holy Trinity? Consider Romans 9:20 and Paul's imagery of the molded pot questioning the molder, the Creator Himself.

4. Review on page 72 the distinction made between the theology of glory and the theology of the cross. An insightful theologian has noted that God uses the little, the least, and the lost to do His work. Or, in other words, God doesn't do His work the Las Vegas-way with lots of bright lights and shows. God continually uses the commonplace, everyday things—and people—of His creation to accomplish His will and work. He uses His First Article gifts to accomplish His Second and Third Article work. All of these God uses to bring us to His Christ-centered gifts of forgiveness. List some ordinary things and people God has used and still uses to bring about His cross-centered will and purpose in Christ.

Ponder

5. When we become preoccupied with the unanswered "whys" and "hows" of theology, we may be led away from the cross of Christ. Despite our unanswered questions, beholding Christ on the cross for the forgiveness of our sins gives us the reassuring answer, "This is sufficient for my faith in Christ. This enough for me." What examples can you think of where people have been led away from Jesus by becoming obsessed with the "whys" and "hows" of God's Word?

Pray

O Incarnate Word, who was made flesh for our redemption, continue to spread abroad the proclamation of Your great work of salvation and also to strengthen my faith. To You, O Jesus, we ask this and pray. Amen.

> **HYMN**
>
> O Word of God incarnate,
> O Wisdom from on high,
> O Truth unchanged, unchanging,
> O Light of our dark sky:
> We praise You for the radiance
> That from the hallowed page,
> A lantern to our footsteps,
> Shines on from age to age.
> —"O Word of God Incarnate"
> (*LSB* 523:1)

CHAPTER 8

What is the Church?
pp. 73–81

BELIEVE, TEACH, CONFESS

I believe that there is upon earth a little holy group and congregation of pure saints, under one head, even Christ [Ephesians 1:22]. This group is called together by the Holy Spirit in one faith, one mind, and understanding, with many different gifts, yet agreeing in love, without sects or schisms [Ephesians 4:5–8, 11]. I am also a part and member of this same group, a sharer and joint owner of all the goods it possesses [Romans 8:17]. I am brought to it and incorporated into it by the Holy Spirit through having heard and continuing to hear God's Word [Galatians 3:1–2], which is the beginning of entering it. (LC II 51–52)

Key Bible Verse:

And [Jesus] is the head of the body, the church. (Colossians 1:18)

Review

1. Ephesians 5:25–27 is quoted on page 73. These are some of the most beautiful words said about and to the Church. List at least five words or phrases used to describe Christ's Bride.

_____

_____

_____

_____

_____

_____

2. On pages 74 and 75 the Church is described in the language of the Nicene Creed. (See page 19 for the full text of the Creed.) In each of the following Bible passages, match the verses with the creedal words used to describe the Church: one, holy, Christian, and apostolic.

Psalm 133:1 _____

1 Peter 3:8 _____

Isaiah 4:2–6 _____

Romans 11:13–16 _____

Acts 11:22–26 _____

1 Peter 4:16 _____

Acts 2:42 _____

Revelation 21:14 _____

3. Three more parts of the Church are described on page 76. The Church is universal, triumphant, and militant. The Church is also described in narrow and broad terms (See pages 76–77 for a review of these terms). Search each of the following Bible passages and determine which verse in each pair fits the narrow or the broad definition of Church.

	Narrow	Broad	
Universal	_____	_____	Galatians 1:1–5 or Revelation 7:9–10
Triumphant	_____	_____	Psalm 59:1–10 or 1 John 4:1–4
Militant	_____	_____	1 Timothy 6:11–12 or Revelation 12:7–11

Connect

4. The choice of churches in today's world is dizzying. What criteria are helpful in choosing a church? See pages 79–81. How were you brought into the congregation to which you now belong?

Ponder

5. The parable of the Pharisee and tax collector in light of justification was considered in the study questions for Chapter 4. Now we look at the same parable in terms of hypocrisy. Review the definition of a hypocrite on page 77. Read Isaiah 19:13 and Luke 18:9–14.

a. According to the definition on page 77, Luke 18:9, and Isaiah 29:13, what are the qualifications for being a hypocrite?

b. What do the Pharisee and the tax collector have in common?

c. Is there a place in the Church for hypocrites? Is there room for you?

Pray

O Christ, whose body is the Church, thank You for making me a part of Your body where You wash me, feed me, and forgive me. Keep me always a member of the one true faith, and heal all divisions that rend unity here on earth. To You, Lord Jesus, do I pray. Amen.

HYMN

I love Your kingdom, Lord,
The place of Your abode,
The Church our blest Redeemer saved
With His own precious blood.
I love Your Church, O God,
Your saints in ev'ry land,
Dear as the apple of Your eye
And graven on Your hand.
—"I Love Your Kingdom, Lord"
(*LSB* 651:1, 3)

CHAPTER 9

It's All about Jesus
Part 3 pp. 82–85

BELIEVE, TEACH, CONFESS

This is our teaching, faith, and confession on this subject: in spiritual matters the understanding and reason of mankind are ‹completely› blind and by their own powers understand nothing, as it is written in 1 Corinthians 2:14, "The natural person does not accept the things of the Spirit of God, for they are folly to him, and he is not able to understand them because they are spiritually discerned." (FC Ep II 2)

Key Bible Verses

For the simple are killed by their turning away,
and the complacency of fools destroys them;
but whoever listens to me will dwell secure
and will be at ease, without dread of disaster. (Proverbs 1:32–33)

Review

1. Turn to Chapter 3 (pp. 36–42) and Chapter 4 (pp. 43–44). Review each chapter in order to prepare for the study of Chapter 9.

Three important points from Chapter 3:
1. Jesus alone was born of a virgin birth and is God's only-begotten Son (pp. 38–39).
2. Jesus alone has lived and accomplished perfect work for our salvation (pp. 39–40).
3. Jesus alone, as God's true Son, is our only Savior (p. 40).

Three important points from Chapter 4:
1. We are sinful to the core of our very being (p. 43).
2. Jesus, who is sinless, took upon Himself our sin (p. 43).
3. This work of Jesus is called justification. It is Jesus' answer to God's wrath over our sin (p. 44).

Connect

2. An important theological word used to describe what happens in the life of a Christian is *regeneration*. The word is synonymous with *justification*, which is explained in Chapter 4. Read Titus 3:4–7 on page 84. In which sacrament does Paul center *regeneration*? Notice the verbs. Verbs are action words. List every action word Jesus does for you.

_____

_____

_____

_____

3. In Martin Luther's hymn on the Lord's Prayer, "Our Father, Who from Heaven Above," the reformer teaches us that conversion falls under the First Petition of the Lord's Prayer, "Hallowed be Thy

Name." Sing or speak the following hymn stanza:

Your name be hallowed. Help us, Lord, / In purity to keep Your Word,

That to the glory of Your name / We walk before You free from blame.

Let no false teaching us pervert; / All poor deluded souls convert. (*LSB* 766:2)

What is the connection between God's name being hallowed and the conversion of an unbeliever?

Ponder

4. Some in the Reformed tradition ardently believe they have made a decision for Jesus. They believe they have already done a good work to save themselves. Roman Catholics believe they can still do good works to save themselves. How do Lutherans explain what they have done to save themselves? See the following Scripture passages for help: Hebrews 10:1–10; Matthew 1:21; Colossians 2:13; Ephesians 2:1–9.

5. A friend gives you one million dollars—a free gift, no strings attached. You exclaim, "Wow! You should have seen how I accepted that one million dollars! I mean, I took it into my own hands and put the money in my own pocket. I did a really great job of taking that gift." What is wrong with this scenario? Consider what Jesus has given to you and rewrite this scenario in a Lutheran way.

> **HYMN**
>
> May God bestow
>   on us His grace,
> With blessings rich provide us;
> And may the brightness of His face
> To life eternal guide us,
> That we His saving health may
>   know,
> His gracious will and pleasure,
> And also to the nations show
> Christ's riches without measure
> And unto God convert them.
> —"May God Bestow on Us His
>   Grace" (*LSB* 824:1)

Pray

O Lord, whose life-giving Word has made me alive, speedily send forth the Spirit to make alive also those who still live in darkness and death. In Your mighty name I pray, O Jesus. Amen.

Putting It All Together:
Lutheran Spirituality
pp. 87–91

Looking it up

1. Read Luke 18:1–34. Note the opening words to this chapter, "And [Jesus] told them a parable to the effect that they ought always to pray and not lose heart." Part of spirituality is prayer. Prayer is stirred by the Word of God and by the Holy Spirit. Prayer is speaking to the Father through the interceding of the Son with words grasping hold of God's multitude of promises. These verses of Luke 18 can be divided into five parts. Reread each section and describe the spirituality of each person or persons.

Spirituality of the persistent (18:1–8)

Spirituality of the forgiven (18:9–14)

Spirituality of children (18:15–17)

Spirituality of the living dead (18:18–30)

Spirituality of the Savior (18:31–34)

Linking it up

2. As the Reformation moved forward, Pope Paul III called for a general council to be held in Italy. Lutheran rulers debated whether or not to attend, but Martin Luther encouraged them saying that this general council would be another opportunity to speak the truth about what Lutherans believe, teach, and confess. To prepare for the council in Italy, the leaders wanted to be prepared with a document that would state the Lutheran position clearly. Requested of Luther was a document to be presented to Lutheran theologians and lay leaders. Though Luther lay gravely ill in bed, his document was presented to the Smalcaldic League on February 8, 1537. At the time the document was not formally adopted, but forty-four Lutherans signed the bottom line. Over the following years, Luther's Smalcald Articles were highly regarded among the Lutherans. The Smalcald Articles were later added to the Lutheran Church's official confession of faith. Article IV of the Smalcald Articles reads:

> We will now return to the Gospel, which does not give us counsel and aid against sin in only one way. God is superabundantly generous in His grace: First, through the spoken Word, by which the forgiveness of sins is preached in the whole world [Luke 24:45–47]. This is the particular office of the Gospel. Second, through Baptism. Third, through the holy Sacrament of the Altar. Fourth, through the Power of the Keys. Also through the mutual conversation and consolation of brethren, "Where two or three are gathered" (Matthew 18:20) and other such verses [especially Romans 1:12]. (SA III IV)

Who knew God is so rich ("superabundantly generous") in His grace! If, according to page 91, spirituality is also liturgical, how are the facets of the Gospel listed below carried out in a worship setting?

a. the Word

b. Baptism

c. the Sacrament of the Altar

d. the Power of the Keys

e. mutual conversation and consolation

Lifting it up

Almighty God, heavenly Father, You have called me into the work of Your vineyard and lavished upon me Your grace and all manner of spiritual and eternal gifts. Help me to live unto You in humility and patience, to hope in Your pure grace and faithfulness, to abide in Your house, and to praise and magnify Your glorious grace forever; through Christ, our Lord. Amen. (702)

HYMN

Praise, my soul, the
   King of heaven;
To His feet your tribute bring;
Ransomed, healed, restored,
   forgiven,
Evermore His praises sing:
Alleluia, alleluia!
Praise the everlasting King.
Praise Him for His grace and favor
To His people in distress;
Praise Him still the same as ever,
Slow to chide and swift to bless:
Alleluia, alleluia!
Glorious in His faithfulness.
—"Praise, My Soul, the King of
   Heaven" (LSB 793:1–2)

CHAPTER 10

Examples of Faith
pp. 92–94

BELIEVE, TEACH, CONFESS

Our churches teach that the history of saints may be set before us so that we may follow the example of their faith and good works, according to our calling. For example, the emperor may follow the example of David [2 Samuel] in making war to drive away the Turk from his country. For both are kings. But the Scriptures do not teach that we are to call on the saints or to ask the saints for help. Scripture sets before us the one Christ as the Mediator, Atoning Sacrifice, High Priest, and Intercessor [1 Timothy 2:5–6]. He is to be prayed to. He has promised that He will hear our prayer [John 14:13]. This is the worship that He approves above all other worship, that He be called upon in all afflictions. "If anyone does sin, we have an advocate with the Father" (1 John 2:1). (AC XXI 1–4)

Key Bible Verse

Let the heavens praise Your wonders, O Lord, Your faithfulness in the assembly of the holy ones! (Psalm 89:5)

Review

1. Write definitions for the following words:

A saint is . . .

A saint is not . . .

A saint is found . . .

Connect

2. Popular (but faulty) are descriptions of sainted grandmothers watching over the edge of heavenly clouds, of babies who have died being transformed into angels, and of those who have entered their eternal rest in the Lord praying for us or being casually involved in our daily lives. Read the following Scripture passages and make a case for why these are not true:

Romans 8:26–27

1 Timothy 2:1–7

Revelation 7:9–11

Ponder

3. Though the death of loved ones who fall asleep in Jesus is painful for us, Jesus has answered the prayers of His people. Consider Martin Luther's explanation of the words in the Lord's Prayer, "Deliver us from evil." He writes:

> We pray in this petition, in summary, that our Father in heaven would rescue us from every evil of body and soul, possessions and reputation, and finally, when our last hour comes, give us a blessed end, and graciously take us from this valley of sorrow to Himself in heaven. (SC, Seventh Petition).

As you consider your loved ones who have died in the Lord, what comfort does this explanation give you?

Pray

O Lord of the Church's saints, both the seen and the unseen, I praise You for making me one of Your saints. Through Your gracious name, Jesus, I pray. Amen.

HYMN

Like a mighty army
Moves the Church of God;
Brothers, we are treading
Where the saints have trod.
We are not divided,
All one body we,
One in hope and doctrine,
One in charity.

Onward, Christian soldiers,
Marching as to war,
With the cross of Jesus
Going on before.
—"Onward, Christian Soldiers"
  (*LSB* 662:2)

Chapter 11

BELIEVE, TEACH, CONFESS

Therefore, the Church's authority and the State's authority must not be confused. The Church's authority has its own commission to teach the Gospel and to administer the Sacraments [Matthew 28:19–20]. Let it not break into the office of another. Let it not transfer the kingdoms of this world to itself. Let it not abolish the laws of civil rulers. Let it not abolish lawful obedience. Let it not interfere with judgments about civil ordinances or contracts. Let it not dictate laws to civil authorities about the form of society. As Christ says, "My kingdom is not of this world" (John 18:36). Also, "Who made Me a judge or arbitrator over you?" (Luke 12:14). Paul also says, "Our citizenship is in heaven" (Philippians 3:20). And, "The weapons of our warfare are not of the flesh but have divine power to destroy strongholds" (2 Corinthians 10:4).

This is how our teachers distinguish between the duties of these two authorities. They command that both be honored and acknowledged as God's gifts and blessings. (AC XXVIII 12–18)

Who's Got the Power?
pp. 95–100

Key Bible Verse

But our citizenship is in heaven . . . (Philippians 3:20)

Review

1. The flower children of the 1960s had a great aversion to "The Man"—those who exercised authority. What they really loathed was power in the hands of others and the struggles that come with acquiring power. In fact, they wanted some power of their own. Power is gained and grasped. Authority is bestowed and given. Read Matthew 7:28–29; Mark 1:22; 11:27–33. What kind of recognizable authority did people see in Jesus' earthly ministry? What bothered the chief priests, the scribes, and the elders so much?

2. During His trial before Pilate, Jesus made an astounding statement about His own kingdom (John 18:33–37). For what kind of kingdom and king was Pilate looking? What, then, does Jesus' kingdom look like? Read Matthew 28:16–20. What key word does Jesus use to make the distinction between power and authority?

Connect

3. Five Old Testament figures loom large as people of God living under or within secular, pagan governments. Queen Esther risked her life to save her people (see the Book of Esther). Daniel was thrown to the lions (Daniel 6). Shadrach, Meshach, and Abednego were thrown into a fiery furnace (Daniel 3:1–4:3). If you are not familiar with these Old Testament people, take some time to familiarize yourself with them. Describe what happens with their God-centered faith within a secular, hostile government.

4. The authority given by Christ to His Church centers in the forgiveness of sins He gained for us by His death upon His cross. This gift of forgiveness is given and entrusted to pastors as the deliverymen of God's Word and Sacraments to His people (see Chapter 12). The same good news is given to Christ's people who then share with others the great gifts they themselves have been given (see Chapters 32 and 33). What happens in the church or congregation when there is an imbalance between the work of the pastor and the work of the people?

Ponder

5. "The good and gracious will of God is done even without our prayer, but we pray in this petition that it may be done among us also" (SC, Third Petition, Lord's Prayer). What comfort does this bring you when you see evil deeds being carried out, either in church or state? Consider Romans 8:28.

HYMN

Before You, Lord,
  we bow,
Our God who reigns above
And rules the world below,
Boundless in pow'r and love.
Our thanks we bring
In joy and praise,
Our hearts we raise
To You, our King!
Earth, hear your Maker's voice;
Your great Redeemer own;
Believe, obey, rejoice,
And worship Him alone.
Cast down your pride,
Your sin deplore,
And bow before
The Crucified.
—"Before You, Lord, We Bow"
  (LSB 966:1, 4–5)

Pray

O Lord, through whom all authority in heaven and on earth comes, bless the governments of this world with a desire for peace. Watch over all pastors and those in spiritual authority that their offices may bring glory to You and grace to Your people. Give to anyone in a position of authority Your wisdom, and guide their words and actions. To You, O Jesus, do I give praise. Amen.

CHAPTER 12

God's Deliverymen
pp. 101–5

BELIEVE, TEACH, CONFESS

Yet as long as all this (namely, Christ's suffering and death) proclaims God's wrath and terrifies a person, it is still not properly the preaching of the Gospel. It remains the preaching of Moses and the Law, and it is, therefore, an alien work of Christ. Passing through this teaching, Christ arrives at His proper office, that is, to preach grace, console, and give life, which is properly the preaching of the Gospel. (FC Ep V 10)

Key Bible Verse

For you were straying like sheep, but have now returned to the Shepherd and Overseer of your souls. (1 Peter 2:25)

Review

1. As discussed in Chapter 11, pastors receive their authority from God. Pastors are mouthpieces, deliverers of the good gifts of Christ to hurting, sinful people. In fact, pastors are very much like ambassadors in a foreign land. They only deliver the message that the ruler has given them to speak. But the ambassador speaks with the full authority of the ruler, as if that ruler were actually present. Read again Matthew 28:16–20, plus John 20:19–23 and Luke 22:14–23. Note the authority, whether explicit or implied, which is given by Jesus to the disciples and from the disciples to pastors.

Connect

2. In fulfillment of Psalm 23, Jesus announces to us that *He* is the Good Shepherd. Read John 10:1–18. What is the difference between the thieves and robbers (vv. 1, 8, 10), the stranger (v. 5), the hired hand (vv. 12–13), and the under shepherd, that is, the pastor?

3. The Third Commandment with explanation reads:

> Remember the Sabbath day by keeping it holy.
>
> *What does this mean?*
>
> We should fear and love God so that we do not despise preaching and His Word, but hold it sacred and gladly hear and learn it.

In addition, this promise is made in the Rite of Confirmation:

> **P**   Do you intend to continue steadfast in this confession and Church and to suffer all, even death, rather than fall away from it?
>
> **R**   *I do, by the grace of God.* (LSB, p. 273)

What does this mean in light of a pastor who may faithfully proclaim God's Word, rightly divide Law and Gospel, loyally administer the Sacraments, and exercise his office in the care of his flock, but is someone you personally don't like? How might you consider part of this "to suffer all?" Read Ephesians 4:1–6, 32.

> **HYMN**
>
> The gifts of grace
>   and peace
>   From absolution flow;
> The pastor's words are Christ's
>   For us to trust and know.
> Forgiveness that we need
>   Is granted to us there;
> The Lord of mercy sends
>   Us forth in His blest care.
> —"The Gifts of God Freely Given"
>   (LSB 602:3)

4. How do you think pastors might break the Third Commandment?

Ponder

5. Here is a tough, but important, question: People, do you regularly pray for your pastor? Pastors, do you regularly pray for your people? You may or may not choose to share your answer.

6. In addition to the responsibilities of preparing to preach, teaching confirmation and Bible classes, visiting the sick and shut-ins, preparing couples for marriage and families to bury their dead, the pastor also provides pastoral care in situations the parish wouldn't—and at times shouldn't—know. There are late night emergency phone calls, vacations interrupted by crises, the knock at the door from one who needs to talk or confess. Even the pizza delivery guy has an end time to his workday. Does your pastor get at least one day off a week? Does he get adequate vacation and rest time? Does your pastor take advantage of the time provided him?

Pray

O Jesus, Shepherd and Overseer of my soul, I pray You to continue to watch over me, guide me through this life, and keep me safe in Your eternal green pastures. In Your holy and precious name I pray. Amen.

CHAPTER 13

Can't We All Get Along?
pp. 107–10

BELIEVE, TEACH, CONFESS

This is the case: being instructed from the prophetic and apostolic Scriptures, we are sure about our doctrine and Confession. By the grace of the Holy Spirit, our minds and consciences have been confirmed to a greater degree. Therefore, we have thought that this Book of Concord should be published. For it seemed very necessary that, amid so many errors that had arisen in our times, as well as causes of offense, variances, and these long-continued disagreements, there should exist a godly explanation and agreement about all these controversies. It should be derived from God's Word, according to the terms by which the pure doctrine might be distinguished and separated from the false. (Preface to the Christian Book of Concord 22)

Key Bible Verse

Behold, how good and pleasant it is when brothers dwell in unity! (Psalm 133:1)

Review

1. A denomination's confessions state was is essential to their faith. The Lutheran Confessions do this too. What are the essentials that define Lutheranism? See pages 21–22 and 179–183 for some ideas.

2. Read Genesis 3:1. How is the serpent's question, "Did God actually say . . .?" the source of all disunity? Give examples of how the serpent's question is still divides the church.

Connect

3. Jesus wasn't afraid to engage in even and measured debate. Though a long account, read John 7:1–52 and 8:12–59. How would you characterize the tone of the Pharisees? To what do they appeal in their argumentation? To what does Jesus appeal and how does He argue?

Ponder

4. "Celebrating Unity in Diversity" is a popular saying adopted by liberal church bodies from pagan religion. This statement gives shape, then, to their practice of open communion. (The opposite of this is described on page 109.) Read Ephesians 4:1–6 and the compare the above slogan with the following communion hymn stanza:

> One bread, one cup, one body, we, / Rejoicing in our unity,
> Proclaim Your love until You come / To bring Your scattered loved ones home.
> —"Lord, Jesus Christ, We Humbly Pray" (*LSB* 623:4)

Why is such unity so important concerning the Lord's Supper?

5. On national and international levels Lutherans regularly participate in theological dialogue and debate for the sake of the purity of the Gospel. Why is it so difficult to have similar debates and discussions at the local level, between neighboring parishes of different denominations? What would such a debate look like?

Pray

Dearest Jesus, Your precious body, the Church, is divided and torn because of heresy, pride, and a love of unrest. Give to Your Church the ability to speak honestly and openly concerning Your Word. Help me to daily pray for unity, which can only come from You. In Your healing name I pray. Amen.

HYMN

O Lord, let this Your
   little flock,
Your name alone confessing,
Continue in Your loving care,
True unity possessing.
Your sacraments, O Lord,
And Your saving Word
To us, Lord, pure retain.
Grant that they may remain
Our only strength and comfort.
—"Lord Jesus Christ, the Church's Head" (*LSB* 647:2)

CHAPTER 14

What about Women?
pp. 111–13

BELIEVE, TEACH, CONFESS

For it is a far higher thing to honor someone than to love someone, because honor includes not only love, but also modesty, humility, and submission to a majesty hidden in them. (LC I 106)

Key Bible Verse

A gracious woman gets honor. (Proverbs 11:16)

Review

1. Three points are made in "In This Chapter" (p. 111). Reinforce these three points even more by reading these additional Scripture passages.

a. To which woman was the highest honor ever given? How does she receive this distinction? Read Luke 1:26–37; 39–55.

b. In what ways are Christian mothers and teachers influential? Read 2 Timothy 1:5; Luke 2:18–19, 51; Matthew 23:37; 1 Thessalonians 2:7.

c. How is submitting not an inferior action? Read Ephesians 5:15–21.

Connect

2. Consider these additional Scriptures concerning the work of women in the New Testament: Mark 12:41–44, 15:40; Luke 8:1–3; 10:38–42; John 12:1–8; Acts 16:11–15, 40; 17:10–12. What is at the heart of their service?

3. As we look around our society we see women carrying out vocations such as postal workers, judges, high government officials, police officers and fire fighters. The list goes on. Yet, out of all occupations available to women, one is not given to them to do—the Office of the Holy Ministry. Refer to Chapter 11 for a review of God's authority and the authority that exists in the world. What makes articulating the scriptural teaching that only men may serve in the Office of the Holy Ministry so difficult in our society?

Ponder

4. Which is better, to discourage women from going into the Office of the Holy Ministry, or to encourage them to appropriately use their talents in a multitude of other ways?

5. On pages x–xxiii in *Lutheran Service Book*, note the recognition accorded many women in the life of Jesus and in the life of the Church. Study *LSB* 518, "By All Your Saints in Warfare," stanzas 20 and 22, and also *LSB* 855, "For All the Faithful Women." Choose one woman to research. Come back to a future session and share what you learned about this sainted woman.

Pray

Lord Jesus, throughout Your earthly ministry You attended to women in need and You also received their friendship and support. Restore to Your Church to a proper understanding of all roles and vocations of all God's people so that Your Word may be honored and Your Church advanced in truth. In Your all-loving name I pray. Amen.

> **HYMN**
>
> Praise God with acclamation
> And in His gifts rejoice.
> Each day finds its vocation
> Responding to His voice.
> Soon years on earth are past;
> But time we spend expressing
> The love of God brings blessing
> That will forever last!
> —"From God Can Nothing Move Me" (*LSB* 713:5)

The Means of Grace

What you'll learn about:

- The Scriptures are God's holy, inspired Word by which He creates and sustains faith.

- God's Word is divided into two great doctrines: Law and Gospel.

- The distinction between Law and Gospel is vital for correctly understanding Scripture.

- God gives the Sacraments to His people for their forgiveness, life, and salvation.

- When one is baptized, he or she is joined to the death and resurrection of Jesus Christ.

- Repentance defines the Christian life and occurs in the very concrete practice of Confession and Absolution.

- Jesus is really present in His body and blood in the bread and wine of the Lord's Supper.

CHAPTER 15

A Word about God's Word pp. 116–25

BELIEVE, TEACH, CONFESS

We, too, are simply to believe with all humility and obedience our Creator and Redeemer's plain, firm, clear, solemn words and command, without any doubt and dispute about how it agrees with our reason or is possible. For these words were spoken by that Lord who is infinite Wisdom and Truth itself. He can do and accomplish everything He promises. (FC SD VII 47)

Key Bible Verse

The crowd was pressing in on [Jesus] to hear the word of God. (Luke 5:1)

Review

1. When you open up a Bible, there are words everywhere—literally chapter and verse. A literate person can easily make sense of the sentences, though once in a while some challenging names pop up. But what does the Bible mean? Unlike any other book in the world, here is a story that spans ages and authors, the rise and fall of civilizations, a story centuries old, and yet a story that has something to say to readers today. There is something living, something about the Savior, something for you.

Review "The Bible Is Different from Any Other Book" on page 124. Look up the following passages to see what God's Word is and what it is not.

Genesis 1:3

1 John 1:5

Psalm 58:3

Isaiah 55:7–9

Matthew 15:19

Matthew 7:18–29

Ephesians 1:13

Connect

2. God's Word creates light. His Word creates faith. His Word sustains life. Choose one of the following readings and study how God's Word creates faith in dark, lifeless hearts. In each case what work did the Word of God and the Holy Spirit do?

John 4:1–41, the woman at the well:

Luke 19:1–10, Zacchaeus:

Matthew 27:38–44; Luke 23:32–43, the thief on the cross:

> **HYMN**
>
> God's Word is our
>   great heritage
> And shall be ours forever;
> To spread its light from age to age
> Shall be our chief endeavor.
> Through life it guides our way,
> In death it is our stay.
> Lord, grant, while worlds endure,
> We keep its teachings pure
> Throughout all generations.
> —"God's Word Is Our Great
>   Heritage" (*LSB* 582)

3. The following is a much-loved collect of the Church.

> Blessed Lord, You have caused all Holy Scriptures to be written for our learning. Grant that we may so hear them, read, mark, learn, and inwardly digest them that, by patience and comfort of Your holy Word, we may embrace and ever hold fast the blessed hope of everlasting life; through Jesus Christ, our Lord. (148)

a. Look up the following passages and match them with the words *hear, read, mark, learn,* and *inwardly digest*: Joshua 8:35; Ezra 7:10; Ezekiel 3:3; Matthew 11:29.

b. How is *hear, read, mark, learn,* and *inwardly digest* a good plan for studying God's Word?

Ponder

4. Jesus' apostles lived their very lives as if they depended solely on the Word of God. See the death of John the Baptist (Matthew 14:1–11); the death of Stephen (Acts 7:54–8:2); and the death of James and the imprisonment of Peter (Acts 12:1–5). If these men had perpetuated a lie concerning the life, death and resurrection of Jesus, would they have died for it? Would you die for a lie? Why is it important to you that God's Word is true?

5. Consider again the key Bible verse above. What gets in the way of people "pressing in on" Jesus in order to hear His Word? What draws people to Jesus so that He might "press" in on them? How does Jesus "press" Himself upon you?

Pray

Pray again the collect in Question 3.

CHAPTER 16

BELIEVE, TEACH, CONFESS

These two doctrines [of Law and Gospel], we believe and confess, should always be diligently taught in God's Church forever, even to the end of the world. They must be taught with the proper distinction of which we have heard: (a) through the preaching of the Law and its threats in the ministry of the New Testament the hearts of impenitent people may be terrified, and (b) they may be brought to a knowledge of their sins and to repentance. This must not be done in such a way that they lose heart and despair in this process. . . . People must be comforted and strengthened again by the preaching of the Holy Gospel about Christ, our Lord. In other words, to those who believe the Gospel, God forgives all their sins through Christ, adopts them as children for His sake, and out of pure grace—without any merit on their part—justifies and saves them. (FC SD V 24–25)

Law and Gospel: The Two Great Doctrines of the Bible pp. 127–34

Key Bible Verse

For Christ is the end of the law for righteousness to everyone who believes. (Romans 10:4)

Review

1. Are you ready to divide some Law and Gospel? Look up the following Scripture passages and write which phrases of the passages are Law and which are Gospel. Carefully watch what you are to do and what you haven't done according to the Law and what God in Christ Jesus has done for you according to the Gospel.

John 1:17

Law:

Gospel:

Romans 5:15b

Law:

Gospel:

Isaiah 6:5, 7

Law:

Gospel:

Connect

2. A friend slips into your cubicle at work. He is crestfallen and visibly upset. "Last night was not good. I was beat when I got home from work. The kids were picking on one another. My wife was up to her eyeballs in dirty laundry. It didn't take long before I blew up. Everyone else ended up in tears. I feel so bad. What do I do now?" Does this friend need to hear Law or Gospel? What are some dangers in speaking to this person's situation? What words do you proclaim?

3. The Law identifies, labels, and tags sin. The Gospel brings healing and life. To apply the Law takes laser-sharp skill. Equal ability is needed to administer the balm of the Gospel. What is the danger of preaching Law and no Gospel? What is the danger of preaching Gospel and no Law? See also pages 132–133 for guidance.

4. The third use of the Law is the joyful response of the hurting and dead heart made alive and healed by the Gospel of Jesus Christ. Consider the following passages and identify those parts that are the third use of the Law. See pages 131–32 for assistance.

Romans 6:4

Galatians 5:1

Hebrews 12:3

1 John 3:16

Ponder

5. Take time to study the hymns "The Law of God Is Good and Wise" (LSB 579) and "The Gospel Shows the Father's Grace" (LSB 580). These two hymns clearly teach the two great doctrines of the Bible. Which stanza of LSB 579 sings of the third use of the Law? Does this hymn end with the Law or the Gospel? Which stanzas of LSB 580 would be appropriate to give to the friend in question 2?

6. Whenever possible, read through the three appointed Scripture readings—the Old Testament, Epistle, and Gospel—before they are read in the worship service. Look carefully in each reading for Law and Gospel. When the readings are read, listen again with your understanding of the Law and Gospel. When the sermon is preached, listen just as carefully for specific, cutting Law and healing, soothing Gospel. Compliment your pastor when he rightly divides Law and Gospel. Remain diligent in your own work of learning to rightly divide Law and Gospel. That last, by the way, is a sentence of sanctification!

Pray

O Christ, the Law clearly shows me my sin, and the Gospel shows me Your love on the cross for me. Teach me to hear Your entire Word and take it to heart. In Your precious name I pray, O Jesus. Amen.

> **HYMN**
>
> The Law reveals the
>   guilt of sin
> And makes us conscience-stricken;
> But then the Gospel enters in
> The sinful soul to quicken.
> Come to the cross, trust Christ, and
>   live;
> The Law no peace can ever give,
> No comfort and no blessing.
> —"Salvation unto Us Has Come"
>   (LSB 555:8)

CHAPTER 17

Delivered in Water
pp. 135–38

Key Bible Verse

Baptism . . . now saves you. (1 Peter 3:21)

BELIEVE, TEACH, CONFESS

Concerning Baptism, our churches teach that Baptism is necessary for salvation [Mark 16:16] and that God's grace is offered through Baptism [Titus 3:4–7]. They teach that children are to be baptized [Acts 2:38–39]. Being offered to God through Baptism, they are received into God's grace. (AC IX:1–2)

Review

1. Study the suggested passages on Baptism, pp. 16–17. Read also the Apostles' Creed on p. 16, which is the creed of Baptism. Note any parts of Baptism about which you may still have questions.

2. How much water is necessary for a Baptism?

3. The Word of God, in and with the water, creates faith. Write a definition of saving faith. For help see Galatians 3:10–14 and Hebrews 10:19–23. See also pp. 50 and 63–66.

Connect

4. If you have witnessed a Baptism in another denomination, or if you were baptized in another denomination, what differences can you note between Baptism in that tradition and a Baptism in a Lutheran church?

5. How would you explain a Baptism to one who has never seen one? How would you explain the meaning of Baptism?

Ponder

6. Baptism is all about Jesus and all about Jesus for you. Read Romans 6:1–11. List at least three benefits of being baptized into Jesus.

_____

_____

_____

7. One of the great divisions among Christians has to do with the Baptism of infants and small children. Write down the evidence in each of the following Scripture passages that show the forgiveness of sins through Baptism is also for infants and small children: Matthew 18:6; 28:19; Acts 2:38–39; 16:25–34.

8. Though not essential, oftentimes a white robe is given to the person being baptized (see *LSB*, p. 271). Read the passages concerning Baptism and the transfiguration of Jesus (*Lutheranism 101*, p. 13). Now read Matthew 17:1–9 and Revelation 7:9–17. What connections can you make between Baptism and the transfiguration of Jesus?

9. If you have been baptized into Christ, and if heaven is now yours, what comfort do you find in being clothed in white and safe in heaven? For further insight, see Isaiah 1:18 and Matthew 28:3.

> **HYMN**
>
> Baptized into Your name most holy,
> O Father, Son, and Holy Ghost,
> I claim a place, though weak and lowly,
> Among Your saints, Your chosen host.
> Buried with Christ and dead to sin,
> Your Spirit now shall live within.
> —"Baptized into Your Name Most Holy" (*LSB* 590:1)

Pray

O Lord of water and the Word, sustain in me a fervent faith that I may more boldly grasp the cleansing blessings of Baptism. In Your name, O Lord Jesus, I pray. Amen.

CHAPTER 18

Confession Is Good for the Soul pp. 139–45

BELIEVE, TEACH, CONFESS

It is well known that we have made clear and praised the benefit of Absolution and the Power of the Keys. Many troubled consciences have derived comfort from our teaching. They have been comforted after they heard that it is God's command, no, rather the very voice of the Gospel, that we should believe the Absolution and regard it as certain that the forgiveness of sins is freely granted to us for Christ's sake. We should believe that through this faith we are truly reconciled to God. This belief has encouraged many godly minds and, in the beginning, brought Luther the highest praise from all good people. This belief shows consciences sure and firm comfort. (Ap XI 59)

Key Bible Verse

I said, "I will confess my transgressions to the Lord," and you forgave the iniquity of my sin. (Psalm 32:5)

Review

1. Find in this chapter one definition for each of the following words. You may expand your definitions with more information found throughout the chapter.

Repentance

Confession

Absolution

2. How might your pastor assist you in repentance, confession, and absolution?

Connect

3. There are several forms of Confession and Absolution in the hymnal. Compare and contrast the following rites. Who speaks and who hears the Confession? Who speaks and who hears the Absolution?

LSB, pp. 184–85

LSB, p. 254

LSB, pp. 290–91

LSB, pp. 292–93

4. Read Luke 5:17–26. What most surprises—and bothers—the Pharisees and the teachers of the Law? Which healing was most important? Which healing does Jesus promise to all sinners, the healing of body or the healing of soul? See Psalm 103:2–5.

Ponder

5. Your pastor's ears are open to hear your confession while his mouth is closed. Your pastor's mouth is open to speak to you absolution while his ears are now stopped with your sins entombed. What comfort is yours to know that your pastor may hear your confession but beyond the confessional, may never speak of your sins? Read Psalm 103:12.

6. Think silently about which sins trouble you the most. What would it take for you to confess them privately to your pastor? Read Isaiah 1:18 and Psalm 31:1–5, 9–10, 14–16, 21–24. Does such cleanness and healing appeal to you?

Pray

Lord, there is nothing in my heart that You cannot see or know. Such dark sins burden me. Stir up in me true repentance, open my mouth to confess these sins, and open my ears to hear the forgiveness won for me by Your death upon the cross. In Your name, O Jesus, I pray. Amen.

HYMN

There is a balm in
    Gilead
To make the wounded whole;
There is a balm in Gilead
To heal the sin-sick soul.
—"There Is a Balm in Gilead"
    (*LSB* 749: Refrain)

CHAPTER 19

BELIEVE, TEACH, CONFESS

Consider this true, almighty Lord, our Creator and Redeemer, Jesus Christ, after the Last Supper. He is just beginning His bitter suffering and death for our sins. In those sad last moments, with great consideration and solemnity, He institutes this most venerable Sacrament. It was to be used until the end of the world with great reverence and obedience ‹humility›. It was to be an abiding memorial of His bitter suffering and death and all His benefits. It was a sealing ‹and confirmation› of the New Testament, a consolation of all distressed hearts, and a firm bond of unity for Christians with Christ, their Head, and with one another. In ordaining and instituting the Holy Supper He spoke these words about the bread, which He blessed and gave: "Take, eat; this is My body, which is given for you," and about the cup, or wine: "This is My blood of the new testament, which is shed for you for the forgiveness of sins." (FC SD VII 44)

The Lord's Supper: Given for You

pp. 147–53

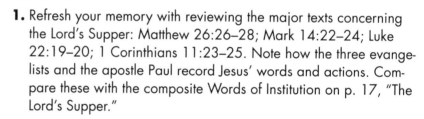

Key Bible Verse

"This is My body, which is given for you." (Luke 22:19)

Review

1. Refresh your memory with reviewing the major texts concerning the Lord's Supper: Matthew 26:26–28; Mark 14:22–24; Luke 22:19–20; 1 Corinthians 11:23–25. Note how the three evangelists and the apostle Paul record Jesus' words and actions. Compare these with the composite Words of Institution on p. 17, "The Lord's Supper."

2. Look at the definition of a sacrament on page 147 and how Jesus fulfills that definition. What are some ways this definition and Jesus' fulfillment are denied or emptied of their meaning?

Connect

3. If you have observed the Lord's Supper in a different denomination, describe some of the things you have seen and heard in a Lutheran Divine Service that were added or taken away in the non-Lutheran service.

4. You have coffee one day with two friends. One says, "We had a great communion service yesterday. The bread and the wine really symbolized our unity as a congregation." The other friend responds, "Unity? When I go to communion it's just about me and Jesus. I go for me." How do you respond to both friends?

Ponder

5. No Jesus, no real presence in the Lord's Supper. No real presence in the Lord's Supper, no Jesus. What is lost to you if there is no Jesus in the Lord's Supper and there is no Jesus "for you?"

6. When you consider your own sinful flesh, your own sinful mind, and your own sinful heart, what benefits do you see from receiving the body and blood of your Lord Jesus? Consider the following Scripture passages: Romans 8:1–11; Psalm 16:9; Romans 12:1–2; Philippians 2:5–11; 2 Corinthians 4:16.

Pray

   O Lord, whose body and blood are given to eat and to drink, drive away all doubt concerning Your real presence in Your supper. Through this holy meal assure me of Your forgiveness of all my sins. In Your name, O Lord Jesus, I pray. Amen.

> **HYMN**
>
> We eat this bread
>   and drink this cup,
> Your precious Word believing
> That Your true body and Your blood
> Our lips are here receiving.
> This Word remains forever true,
> All things are possible with You,
> For You are Lord Almighty.
> Though reason cannot understand,
> Yet faith this truth embraces:
> Your body, Lord, is even now
> At once in many places.
> I leave to You how this can be;
> Your Word alone suffices me;
> I trust its truth unfailing.
> —"Lord Jesus Christ, You Have
>   Prepared" (*LSB* 622:4–5)

CHAPTERS 20 AND 21

BELIEVE, TEACH, CONFESS

But what should you do if you are not aware of this need and have no hunger and thirst for the Sacrament?

To such a person no better advice can be given than this: first, he should touch his body to see if he still has flesh and blood. Then he should believe what the Scriptures say of it in Galatians 5 and Romans 7. Second, he should look around to see whether he is still in the world, and remember that there will be no lack of sin and trouble, as the Scriptures say in John 15–16 and in 1 John 2 and 5. Third, he will certainly have the devil also around him, who with his lying and murdering day and night will let him have no peace, within or without, as the Scriptures picture him in John 8 and 16; 1 Peter 5; Ephesians 6; and 2 Timothy 2. (SC, Christian Questions, 20)

The Lord's Supper: Dinners with Sinners

pp. 154–58

Key Bible Verse

And the Pharisees and the scribes grumbled, saying, "This man receives sinners and eats with them." (Luke 15:2)

Review

1. When the altar is prepared for the Lord's Supper, sooner or later the questions will arise in one's mind: "Should I go or shouldn't I? Am I ready? Am I prepared?" Look at pages 155–56. List three points to be considered when preparing to go to the Lord's Supper.

Connect

2. The Lord's Supper is often called "the marriage feast of the Lamb." Read Jesus' parable of the wedding feast in Matthew 22:1–14. Remember as you read that at the heart of this parable is the Gospel, the gracious invitation from the king to attend his feast. But there is also the application of the Law when the invitation is rejected by many and when one attendee is found ill-prepared. Focus on v. 12. Why is the man thrown out? Why is he speechless? What could the man have said to the king?

Ponder

3. The Lord Jesus loves to eat with His people. Not only does Jesus extend this invitation to you, and not only does He prepare and serve the food—His body, His blood—but Jesus makes certain you are clean (baptized) and well-dressed in His white robe of righteousness. What comfort and hope do you find in the following statement, "Perfect people do not come to the Lord's Supper, but the perfect Lord Jesus serves His perfect body and blood to you."

The Lord's Supper: The Lord's Care
pp. 160–63

Key Bible Verse

And they devoted themselves to the apostles' teaching and the fellowship, to the breaking of bread and the prayers. (Acts 2:42)

Review

1. Summarize the reasons why Lutherans only commune at the altars of Lutherans with the same beliefs.

Connect

2. This chapter speaks of family traditions within the context of meals. One such tradition is the bringing of children to the communion rail for a blessing. What are some of the benefits of such a tradition? See Exodus 12:21–17; Deuteronomy 6:20–25; Psalm 78:1–8.

Ponder

3. Read Matthew 11:28. Reflecting this Scripture passage, a communion hymn dear to many Lutherans begins with these words, "I come, O Savior, to Thy table, For weak and weary is my soul" (*LSB* 618:1). What weaknesses will you bring to the Lord's Table the next time you attend His Supper?

Pray

O Jesus, both Lord of Your Table and Your Church, prepare my heart to commune rightly even as I pray for those who do not yet understand the presence of Your body and blood. Heal our divisions and give us hope for unity in Your Body, the Church. In Your healing name I pray. Amen.

HYMN

Weary am I and
  heavy laden;
With sin my soul is sore oppressed;
Receive me graciously and gladden
My heart, for I am now Thy guest.
Lord, may Thy body and Thy blood
Be for my soul the highest good!
—"I Come, O Savior, to Thy Table"
  (*LSB* 618:4)

PART FOUR

Lutherans at a Glance

What you'll learn about:

- The Reformation arose out of Martin Luther's concern about how the Church thought and taught about salvation.

- How politics and theology in the 1500s influenced each other and became the seedbed of the Reformation.

- The Book of Concord contains the official confession of the Lutheran Church and is the standard by which all doctrine and practice is determined to be correct.

- Lutherans came to America during the colonial period and saw another great period of immigration between the 1850s and the 1900s.

- When Lutherans came to the New World, they brought with them a passion for education of the young, including religious instruction.

CHAPTERS 22 AND 23

BELIEVE, TEACH, CONFESS

Our churches are now, through God's grace, enlightened and equipped with the pure word and right use of the Sacraments, with knowledge of the various callings and right works. (SA Preface 10)

Luther: The Unlikely Reformer and The World of the Reformation pp. 166–78

Key Bible Verse

For I decided to know nothing among you except Jesus Christ and Him crucified. (1 Corinthians 2:2)

Review

1. List five errors Martin Luther saw in the Church. See the section "Here I Stand" on page 168. See also page 178 for further help.

_____

_____

_____

_____

_____

2. As she is scattered throughout the world in various Christian denominations and traditions, where in the Church are the above errors still an issue?

Connect

3. Excommunication is the church rite of bringing the most extreme form of spiritual discipline upon an unrepentant person. In the Middle Ages this was even given sensory finality. A bell was rung as if the person being excommunicated had died. The Book of Gospels was closed, indicating that the Gospel, especially the forgiveness of sins, had no place in the person's life until repentance was wrought by the Law. Finally, a candle was snuffed out, showing the person to be in utter darkness. Although these were not done for or to Martin Luther, how did Luther treat his own excommunication? See page 169. Ask your pastor to show you the Rite of Excommunication used in the Lutheran Church.

4. Discuss the two important discoveries which occurred in the 1400s, the discovery of the New World (p. 173) and the discovery or invention of movable type (p .174). What benefits did the Reformation reap from this invention and this event?

Ponder

5. Consider again the Key Bible Verse at the beginning of this study. What evidence is there that Jesus Christ and Him crucified was at the heart of Luther's life and the Reformation?

Pray

O Lord who changes not, in this world full of sin and corruption, bring Your never-changing Word to bear upon heresy and unbelief that Your truth may reach to the ends of the earth. O Christ, in Your name we pray. Amen.

HYMN

I am trusting Thee,
   Lord Jesus,
Trusting only Thee;
Trusting Thee for full salvation,
Great and free.
—"I Am Trusting Thee, Lord Jesus"
   (*LSB* 729:1)

Putting It All Together:
Confession of Faith
pp. 179–83

Looking it up

The Lutheran Confessions are called so because of their source and commitment to God's Word. Lutherans are to confess solely the holy, infallible Word of God. The Lutheran Confessions stand true as the day they were written because they are based on the eternal Word of God.

Read Matthew 16:13–19. These words are foundational to the Roman Catholic Church for the existence of the papacy. There are two important words in the central verse:

> "And I tell you, you are Peter [*Petros*], and on this rock [*petra*] I will build my church, and the gates of hell shall not prevail against it." (Matthew 16:18)

Jesus makes a play on words, Peter's name versus the confession of faith Peter makes, that is, that Jesus is the Son of the living God. Who is the source of Peter's confession?

Linking it up

"The Power and Primacy of the Pope" is perhaps the least known of the Lutheran confessional documents, though its title certainly is memorable. With a need to clearly define the Lutherans' issues with the papacy, Philip Melanchthon wrote this document against the power and primacy of the pope in 1537 at the same time the Smalcald Articles were being written by Martin Luther.

Read Matthew 7:24–27. What—or who—is the rock upon which the house is built? See also Psalm 18:2, 31; Exodus 17:1–7; and 1 Corinthians 10:1–4.

With great care, then, do the Lutherans approach the prickly task of defining the authority of Christ against the self-appointed earthly and heavenly rule of the papacy. What is the big deal? Jesus, the Son of God, is your Rock-sized Savior, and *that* is a big deal!

Lifting it up

Almighty and everlasting God, You have given us grace to acknowledge the glory of the eternal Trinity by the confession of a true faith and to worship the Unity in the power of the Divine Majesty. Keep us steadfast in this faith and defend us from all adversities; for You, O Father, Son, and Holy Spirit, live and reign, one God, now and forever. Amen. (L52)

HYMN

My hope is built on
    nothing less
Than Jesus' blood and
    righteousness;
No merit of my own I claim
But wholly lean on Jesus' name.
On Christ, the solid rock, I stand;
All other ground is sinking sand.
—"My Hope Is Built on Nothing
    Less (*LSB* 576:1, refrain)

CHAPTERS 24 AND 25

Lutheranism after Luther and Changes and Challenges to Lutheranism pp. 184–94

BELIEVE, TEACH, CONFESS

By the Almighty's special grace and mercy, the teaching about the chief articles of our Christian religion (which under the papacy had been horribly clouded by human teachings and ordinances) had been explained and purified again from God's Word by Dr. Luther, of blessed and holy memory. . . . We intend also, by the Almighty's grace, to abide faithfully by this Christian Confession . . . until our death just as it was delivered in the year 1530 to Emperor Charles V. (FC SD Introduction 1, 5)

Key Bible Verse

Your kingdom is an everlasting kingdom,
and Your dominion endures throughout all generations.
The LORD is faithful in all His words
and kind in all His works. (Psalm 145:13)

Review

1. The people who inherited from Martin Luther the beginnings of the Reformation needed a name. Should they be called "Lutherans" or should they be called "Evangelicals?" What were the pros and cons for each name? See pages 169 and 184 and 1 Corinthians 1:10–13a.

2. As the Reformation matured it was challenged by two movements from with in the ranks of the reformers, Pietism and Rationalism. In short, Pietism emphasizes the heart or emotions. Rationalism emphasizes the brain or human intellect. See page 188 for more detailed definitions. Where do you see these two movements in today's American Christianity?

Connect

3. At the miracle of Pentecost the apostles spoke in the same tongues as the multitude of Jews speaking more than fourteen different languages. As Lutherans immigrated to the United States, they brought their own languages. Often synods were formed around the European country of origin and the native language of the now-American Lutherans. Historically, the predominant language of The Lutheran Church—Missouri Synod was German. How was this an advantage and a disadvantage to the proclamation of the Gospel of Jesus? See pages 190–92 for guidance.

Ponder

4. Since the Reformation began there has been more fracturing of the Church (see p. 186) and there has been movement toward unity, whether real or imagined (see pp. 191–94). Review also Chapter 13. Read Acts 2:42. What are the four foundations to have God-pleasing unity?

_____

_____

_____

_____

Pray

   Dear Christ our Savior, You purify our faith as gold in the fire. Test us not beyond what we can bear but press from us only that which bears glory to Your name and hope to the world. In Your priceless Name we pray. Amen.

HYMN

While life's dark
   maze I tread
And griefs around me spread,
Be Thou my guide;
Bid darkness turn to day,
Wipe sorrow's tears away,
Nor let me ever stray
From Thee aside.
—"My Faith Looks Up to Thee"
   (*LSB* 702:3)

CHAPTER 26

No Lazy Bellies Allowed! pp. 197–200

BELIEVE, TEACH, CONFESS

I beg you all for God's sake, my dear sirs and brethren, who are pastors or preachers, to devote yourselves heartily to your office [1 Timothy 4:13]. Have pity on the people who are entrusted to you [Acts 20:28] and help us teach the catechism to the people, and especially to the young. And let those of you who cannot do better take these tables and forms and impress them, word for word, on the people (Deuteronomy 6:7). (SC, Preface, 6)

Key Bible Verse

For this reason I bow my knees before the Father, from whom every family in heaven and on earth is named. (Ephesians 3:14–15)

Review

1. At the heart of Lutheran education is the Small Catechism. If the head of the household taught the Small Catechism as Luther encouraged, how would this change Christian education in your congregation? What gets in the way of this?

Connect

2. Discuss the ways education today hurts or harms the Church. What can your congregation do to give the very best Christ-centered education to all ages?

Ponder

3. Education is one of the ways the Church raises "sons and daughters" for herself. An elderly women taught Sunday school for fifty years. She never had a husband or children. Through the Word of God, though, countless sons and daughters had become her own. When she died, she left a gift from her estate to her church for they, she said, ". . . were her family." What comfort is there for those who never marry, for those who never have children, or for those who become childless because of the death of children? Read 1 John 2:12–14; 3:1 and James 1:27. How do John and James speak of the Church as "family?"

Pray

O Christ, who once was a child and learned from earthly parents even while knowing all things, impart to us Your knowledge that we may also teach others of many ages. In Your wise name we pray. Amen.

> **HYMN**
>
> Lord Jesus Christ, the children's friend,
> To each of them Your presence send;
> Call them by name and keep them true
> In loving faith, dear Lord, to You.
> In Christian homes, Lord, let them be
> Your blessing to their family;
> Let Christian schools Your work extend
> In living truth as You intend.
> —"Lord Jesus Christ, the Children's Friend" (*LSB* 866:1–2)

PART FIVE

Worship: The Blessings of God

What you'll learn about:

- The Divine Service is the chief worship service among Lutherans.

- The Christian Church Year is used to not only mark time but also to set the story of Jesus in an orderly pattern for teaching.

- The sign of the cross is given to each of us in our Baptism and is used by Lutherans as a token of our salvation.

CHAPTER 27

Finding Meaning in the Words pp. 204–9

BELIEVE, TEACH, CONFESS

The Sacrament, in which faith enlivens terrified hearts, is a service of the New Testament. That is because the New Testament requires spiritual inclinations, making dead and alive. Christ instituted the Sacrament for this use, since He commanded the disciples to do this in remembrance of Him. . . . it is remembering Christ's benefits and receiving them through faith, to be enlivened by them. **(Ap XXIV 71, 72)**

Key Bible Verse

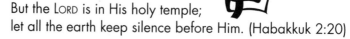

But the LORD is in His holy temple; let all the earth keep silence before Him. (Habakkuk 2:20)

Review

1. Define the following words connected to the "Divine Service." See pages 205–6 for help.

Divine:

Service:

Divine Service:

Worship:

2. The Holy Spirit and the Word of God are inseparable in their work, whether that work is creation (see Genesis 1:1–3) or the creation of faith (see Acts 2). Consider what the Small Catechism says:

"In the same way [the Holy Spirit] calls, gathers, enlightens, and sanctifies the whole Christian church on earth, and keeps it with Jesus Christ in the one true faith." (SC, Third Article)

So, Sunday morning you hit the snooze three times, groggily roll out of a warm bed, stub your toe, shower, get dressed, eat breakfast, warm up the car, drive down empty byways, and pull into a full parking lot. A smiling usher hands you a bulletin and you sit in your favorite pew. How did you get there?

Connect

3. This study's Key Bible Verse teaches us that in worship the earth is silent before the Lord. So it is in the Divine Service. We are silent because God speaks first. God desires to first give His Word to us so that we have something to say back to Him—and a reason to. In addition, the language of worship reflects the language of salvation. (See Chapter 4 for the language of salvation.) Just as we were dead in our sins and God made us alive through His Spirit and Word, so it is at the beginning of every Divine Service. We come once again dead in sin. God speaks and makes us alive through His absolution, His forgiveness. God in Christ Jesus gives gifts.

In faith we receive God's gifts. Study the following Scripture passages. Where the word *receive* or *received* is found, replace it with the word *accept* or *accepted*. Discuss what difference that one word change makes. See Psalm 24:5; Romans 5:17; Hebrews 11:17; and 1 Peter 2:10.

Ponder

4. Turn to pages 206 and 207, "The Divine Service Tells the Story of Salvation." In what way is this outline a helpful approach to understanding the main point of the Divine Service—that the Divine Service is all about Jesus? One of the reasons given by Lutherans for hesitating to invite others to the Divine Service is that such visitors won't understand what's happening. Using the Divine Service as an outline to tell about Jesus, can you think of someone you can invite to worship and use this as an introduction and explanation for what that person will encounter?

Pray

Dear Christ Jesus, Your words are not empty but filled with Your power, Your grace, and Your mercy. As Your Word fills and fleshes out the worship of the Church, may I continue to receive Your gifts, even as I, through faith, return to You thanks and praise. Through the holy name of Father, Son, and Spirit I pray. Amen.

HYMN

God Himself is
    present:
Let us now adore Him
And with awe appear before Him.
God is in His temple;
All within keep silence;
Humbly kneel in deepest rev'rence.
He alone
On His throne
Is our God and Savior;
Praise His name forever!
—"God Himself Is Present"
    (*LSB* 907:1)

CHAPTER 28

Order in the *Order*
pp. 211–21

BELIEVE, TEACH, CONFESS

A ceremony is a sort of picture, or seal, as Paul (Romans 4:11) calls it, the Word making known the promise. Therefore, just as the promise is useless unless it is received through faith, so a ceremony is useless unless faith, which is truly confident that the forgiveness of sins is here offered, is added. (Ap XXIV 70)

Key Bible Verse

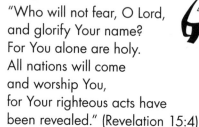

"Who will not fear, O Lord, and glorify Your name? For You alone are holy. All nations will come and worship You, for Your righteous acts have been revealed." (Revelation 15:4)

Note: For this study you will need a copy of Lutheran Service Book.

Review

1. Look through the order of the Divine Service on pages 212–18 in *Lutheranism 101*. Choose one element, such as the Kyrie, and compare that element in the five settings of the Divine Service from *Lutheran Service Book*. Next time you meet with your group, share what differences and similarities you discovered between the five services.

_____

_____

_____

_____

_____

Connect

2. Turn to pages 993–97 of *Lutheran Service Book*. This section of the hymnal is arranged so that you can find hymns according to topic. For instance, if you look at the Advent section, you will notice pages listed in bold type. This is the regular Advent section of hymns. You will also notice more hymns listed below. These hymns first fit a different topic, but they also reflect the season of Advent.

Lutheranism 101 states that "we choose hymns that are doctrinally sound and theologically significant to round out our worship" (p. 211). Look at the Psalm paraphrase section of the topic index in *Lutheran Service Book* (p. 996). Choose one hymn. Look up the psalm upon which the hymn is based and compare the two. Note how the writer reflects the psalm in his hymn version.

Ponder

3. In what ways does the architecture and symbols of your church building communicate God's presence? See pages 220–21 and compare your own church to the classic structure of a place of worship. In your own church are there Christian symbols you don't recognize or understand? Ask your pastor for explanations or look at pages 275–83 in *Luther's Small Catechism with Explanation* for help with interpreting Christian symbols.

4. What is the most difficult part of the Divine Service for you? Discuss in your group and with your pastor possible solutions for easing this difficulty.

5. Ask your pastor what goes into planning and preparing a worship service. How does he or some other appointed person, such as a director of music, choose hymns? How does he decide which readings to use and which to preach on?

Pray

O Lord Jesus, who ordered the universe and Your plan of salvation, so also have You given special attention to how Your Word and the Sacraments come to me. May my heart gratefully receive these gifts from You, and may I rejoice in the worship of Your holy, saving name. In that same name, O Lord Jesus, do I pray. Amen.

HYMN

O worship the King,
all-glorious above.
O gratefully sing
His pow'r and His love;
Our shield and defender,
the Ancient of Days,
Pavilioned in splendor
and girded with praise.
Frail children of dust
and feeble as frail,
In Thee do we trust,
nor find Thee to fail.
Thy mercies, how tender,
how firm to the end,
Our maker, defender,
redeemer, and friend!
—"O Worship the King"
(LSB 804:1, 5)

Putting It All Together:
Nothing Else Than Faith
pp. 222–24

Looking it up

1. The worship of the Church here on earth is heavenly. Read Isaiah 6:1–7; Revelation 7:9–17; 19:6–10. Note how God deals in His most heavenly way with our sin, the effects of sin, and the new life that is ours in Jesus.

2. "So what is Christian worship?" List here for review several of the answers given in this section. Does Scripture's lack of specific direction permit what might be termed an "anything goes" approach to Christian worship?

Linking it up

Religious education in the early years of the Reformation was dark and dreary. In 1529 Martin Luther took what he had observed in pastoral visits and what he had recently preached and put together the Small and Large Catechisms.

From the Small Catechism we read:

> Remember the Sabbath day by keeping it holy. *What does this mean?* Answer: We should fear and love God so that we may not despise preaching and His Word, but hold it sacred, and gladly hear and learn it. (Third Commandment)

From the Large Catechism, we read:

> God's Word is the true "holy thing" above all holy things. Yes, it is the only one we Christians know and have. Though we had the bones of all the saints or all holy and consecrated garments upon a heap, still that would not help us at all. All that stuff is a dead thing that can sanctify no one. But God's Word is the treasure that sanctifies everything [1 Timothy 4:5]. (LC I 91)

In what you have read in the chapters up to this point, how would you summarize worship and the day of worship, the Sabbath?

HYMN

Lord, help us ever
   to retain
The Catechism's doctrine plain
As Luther taught the Word of truth
In simple style to tender youth.
Help us Your holy Law to learn,
To mourn our sin and from it turn
In faith to You and to Your Son
And Holy Spirit, Three in One.
Hear us, dear Father, when we
   pray
For needed help from day to day
That as Your children we may live,
Whom You baptized and so
   received.
Lord, when we fall or go astray,
Absolve and lift us up, we pray;
And through the Sacrament
   increase
Our faith till we depart in peace.
—"Lord, Help Us Ever to Retain"
   (*LSB* 865:1–4)

Lifting it up

Lord, I love the habitation of Your house and the place where Your glory dwells. In the multitude of Your tender mercies prepare my heart that I may enter Your house to worship and confess Your holy name; through Jesus Christ, my God and Lord. (145)

CHAPTER 29

A Time for Everything
pp. 227–30

BELIEVE, TEACH, CONFESS

On this day of rest (since we can get no other chance), we have the freedom and time to attend divine service. We come together to hear and use God's Word, and then to praise God, to sing and to pray [Colossians 3:16]. (LC I 84)

Key Bible Verse

For everything there is a season, and a time for every matter under heaven. (Ecclesiastes 3:1)

Review

1. In Chapter 10, the "saints" of the Church are discussed. Turn to pages x–xiii of *Lutheran Service Book*. First, note the outline of the church year and the scheme of colors indicated. (See 2 Chronicles 2:7 for an Old Testament example of the use of colors.) What are the seasonal colors of the Church Year and what do they signify and teach us?

2. Next, note the Feasts, Festivals, and Commemorations that follow. Why are these dates important?

Connect

3. "Time is of the essence." Those words are used in legal contracts that state a mandatory agreement to specific times and dates. Thankfully we don't live under such a law when using the times appointed for the Church Year. The grace of God abounds and the design of the Church Year is to point us to Jesus. In fact, the season of Advent through the Ascension of the Lord Jesus helps us live out the Second Article of the Apostles' Creed (p. 18). The Church Year becomes a step-by-step living and learning experience for the worshiper. Is the Church Year commanded or forbidden? See Colossians 2:16–17.

Ponder

4. See pages 229–30 for the specific divisions of the Church Year. Do you have a favorite season? Why is this season important to you?

Pray

Jesus, Lord of all, You established the time of earthly seasons, and I thank You for giving me the seasons of the Church Year. As these colors, themes, and dates come and go, help me to always remember You are at the center of all worship. In Your timeless name I pray. Amen.

HYMN

Now the queen of
  seasons, bright
With the day of splendor,
With the royal feast of feasts
Comes its joy to render;
Comes to gladden faithful hearts
Which with true affection
Welcome in unwearied strain
Jesus' resurrection!
—"Come, You Faithful, Raise the
  Strain" (*LSB* 487:3)

CHAPTER 30

The Sign of the Cross
pp. 231–32

BELIEVE, TEACH, CONFESS

In the morning, when you get up, make the sign of the holy cross . . . In the evening, when you go to bed, make the sign of the holy cross and say: **In the name of the Father and of the ✝ Son and of the Holy Spirit. Amen.** *(SC, Morning Prayer and Evening Prayer)*

Key Bible Verse

For in [Jesus] all the fullness of God was pleased to dwell, and through Him to reconcile to Himself all things, whether on earth or in heaven, making peace by the blood of His cross. (Colossians 1:19–20)

Review

1. Do you remember the first time you saw someone make the sign of the cross? What was the setting? What did you think at the time?

Connect

2. A six-year-old boy sits in the pew. He sees his aunt and uncle kneel at the Communion rail. After receiving the body and blood of Jesus, they do something with their right hands. He has only seen this done once, when he went to a wedding at the Roman Catholic parish across the street. Have his aunt and uncle become Roman Catholic too? How would you explain the making of the sign of the cross in the Lutheran Church to a six-year-old?

Ponder

3. What dangers might exist in making the sign of the cross? See p. 231. Do you ever see the sign of the cross being misused?

Pray

O Christ, in Baptism Your cross became my cross. I am marked in Your name and with the sign of Your saving work. May every thought from my head and heart be pleasing to You, for under Your forgiveness do I live. Savior, Jesus, hear my prayer. Amen.

HYMN

In the cross of Christ
   I glory,
Tow'ring o'er the wrecks of time.
All the light of sacred story
Gathers round its head sublime.
—"In the Cross of Christ I Glory"
   (*LSB* 427:1)

PART SIX

Living as Lutherans

What you'll learn about:

- The Church has formulated clear confessions of faith in response to both the lack of faith and attacks on faith.

- The good works we do are a great benefit to our family, friends, neighbors, and all the people with whom we share God's good earth.

- This desire to go tell others about Jesus is the result of the Holy Spirit's work in each believer, and it is at the heart of the Church's mission.

- What we do with our time, talents, and treasures flow from our relationship with God.

CHAPTER 31

BELIEVE, TEACH, CONFESS

I believe in God the Father, who has created me; I believe in God the Son, who has redeemed me; I believe in the Holy Spirit, who sanctifies me. One God and one faith, but three persons. (LC II 7)

We Confess pp. 236–42

Key Bible Verse

Great indeed, we confess, is the mystery of godliness:
He was manifested in the flesh,
vindicated by the Spirit,
seen by angels,
proclaimed among the nations,
believed on in the world,
taken up in glory. (1 Timothy 3:16)

Review

1. Most often the Apostles' Creed, which is the oldest of the three formal creeds and is most closely connected to Baptism in the Early Christian Church, is still confessed at Baptisms, confirmations, and at non-communion services. There is nothing wrong, though, with confessing the Apostles' Creed at a Divine Service. The Nicene Creed is most often confessed at services where the Lord's Supper is celebrated because of its expanded Second Article about Jesus. The Athanasian Creed is typically confessed at least once a year on Trinity Sunday (the only Sunday in the Church Year that is assigned a specific doctrine or teaching of the Church). Some congregations will confess the Athanasian Creed in the worship service when there is a fifth Sunday in the month, which is usually four times a year. With all of that said, we learn there isn't a Sunday that goes by where a creed isn't confessed. Why is there so much emphasis placed on confessing these three creeds?

2. What is the danger of pastors or people writing their own creeds to be used on Sunday mornings or at other times? What is the danger if the Church does away with its three Ecumenical Creeds?

Connect

3. In the study for Chapter 28 you were encouraged to look at a hymn that is a paraphrase of a psalm. Now we compare two hymns that put to music the words of the Apostles' Creed. Review hymns 953 and 954 in *Lutheran Service Book*. These two hymns may be used occasionally as alternatives to the spoken creeds. What phrases in these two hymns help you see from a different perspective God's grace in Christ Jesus?

Ponder

4. One of the most troublesome, though not untrue, statements of the Apostles' Creed is the phrase, "He [Jesus] descended into hell." These words do not show up in the creed until the early fifth century. Because of this late date, some church bodies refuse to confess these words. Read again the paragraph on p. 240 concerning the biblical truth concerning Jesus' descent into hell. Read also the following passages for more assurance that these words in the Apostles' Creed, also contained in the Athanasian Creed, are based on Scripture: Psalm 139; Ephesians 4:1–10; and Colossians 2:8–15. Martin Luther also pointed to Matthew 12:22–32 as a source for this teaching. Why do you think St. Paul in the Ephesians and Colossians passages talks about Baptism before he talks about Jesus' descent into hell? What comfort is yours that Jesus descended into hell *for you*?

Pray

Dear Jesus, every knee shall bow and every tongue confess that You are Lord. May the confession of my own mouth and that of my Church ring bold and true in this world so that many may learn of You and Your saving work for them. In Your name that is above every name I pray. Amen.

HYMN

Holy Father,
    holy Son,
Holy Spirit, three we name Thee;
Though in essence only one,
Undivided God we claim Thee
And, adoring, bend the knee
While we own the mystery.
—"Holy God, We Praise Thy
    Name" (*LSB* 940:5)

CHAPTER 32

We Love God and Our Neighbors pp. 243–46

Key Bible Verse

And let us consider how to stir up one another to love and good works. (Hebrews 10:24)

Review

1. The first time someone failed at loving God and loving the neighbor was in the Garden of Eden. Read Genesis 3:1–19. List the ways Adam and Eve failed to love God. List the ways Adam and Eve failed to love each other.

Connect

2. The Ten Commandments (p. 15) tell you what the good works toward God and your neighbor are. The keeping of these Commandments is the fruit which flows from faith in Christ Jesus. The author of Chapter 32 asks the question, "What kinds of works are good?" (p. 245). These works are expanded by St. Paul in his letters to the Christians in Galatia and Colossae. Read Galatians 5:16–24 and Colossians 3:5–17. Make a list for both the bad fruit and good fruit. Some appear in both letters.

Bad fruit   Good fruit

_____   _____

_____   _____

_____   _____

_____   _____

_____   _____

_____   _____

_____   _____

BELIEVE, TEACH, CONFESS

We cannot boast of many merits and works, if they are viewed apart from grace and mercy. As it is written, "Let the one who boasts, boast in the Lord" (1 Corinthians 1:31); namely, that he has a gracious god. For with that, all is well. We say, besides, that if good works do not follow, the faith is false and not true. (SA III XIII 3–4)

Ponder

3. The author of Chapter 32 makes the wonderful point that God's love for you is His greatest work (p. 243). Read Revelation 22:1–5. What is God's finishing work in heaven for you? How do these words bring you comfort and hope?

4. As we near the end of the studies for *Lutheranism 101*, consider the following words from Hebrews 10:19–25. Not only do these words speak of good works toward your neighbor, but also so much more. Look at the phrases below and match them with the chapters and topics that you have already studied.

- ¹⁹Therefore, brothers, since we have confidence to enter the holy places by the blood of Jesus, ²⁰by the new and living way that He opened for us through the curtain, that is, through His flesh,

  _____

- ²¹and since we have a great priest over the house of God, ²²let us draw near with a true heart in full assurance of faith, _____

- with our hearts sprinkled clean from an evil conscience and our bodies washed with pure water.

  _____

- ²³Let us hold fast the confession of our hope without wavering,

  _____

- for He who promised is faithful. _____

- ²⁴And let us consider how to stir up one another to love and good works,

  _____

- ²⁵not neglecting to meet together, as is the habit of some, but encouraging one another,

  _____

  _____

- and all the more as you see the Day drawing near.

  _____

Pray

O Savior, who loves perfectly and completely, help me to love my neighbor, wherever he or she may be found, whether in my home, at my job, in my neighborhood or as a complete stranger. To You to whom there are no strangers, O Jesus, I pray. Amen.

HYMN

Faith clings to Jesus' cross alone
And rests in Him unceasing;
And by its fruits true faith is known,
With love and hope increasing.
For faith alone can justify;
Works serve our neighbor and supply
The proof that faith is living.
—"Salvation unto Us Has Come"
(*LSB* 555:9)

Putting It All Together:
Living in Two Kingdoms pp. 247–49

Looking it up

1. All of us have multiple vocations in the world in which we live. Explore the following passages and list some of the vocations of Jesus. You may add others as you think of them.

Matthew 13:55

John 11:1–11

John 17:1–5

John 18:33–37

You also have a lively and varied life. Make a list of your many vocations.

_____

_____

_____

_____

_____

_____

_____

Linking it up

2. As God's people live within two kingdoms, they are not without a King. Who is this King who rules over His kingdom? He is one who once wore a crown of thorns on the throne of His cross (Matthew 27:29). He is the one who now has crowns cast before His heavenly throne (Revelation 4:10). His name is Jesus. His vocation as Savior was the humblest of all and yet is the greatest of all. We learn more from the Lutheran Confessions about who this King is:

> Christ always had this majesty according to the personal union. Yet He abstained from using it in the state of His humiliation, and because of this He truly increased in all wisdom and favor with God and men. Therefore, He did not always use this majesty, but only when it pleased Him. Then, after His resurrection, He entirely laid aside the form of a servant, but not the human nature, and was established in the full use, manifestation, and declaration of the divine majesty. In this way

He entered into His glory [Philippians 2:6–11]. So now not just as God, but also as man He knows all things and can do all things. He is present with all creatures, and has under His feet and in His hands everything that is in heaven and on earth and under the earth, as He Himself testifies [in Matthew 28:18], "All authority in heaven and on earth has been given to Me" [see also John 13:3]. And St. Paul says in Ephesians 4:10, "He . . . ascended far above all the heavens, that He might fill all things." Because He is present, He can exercise His power everywhere. To Him everything is possible and everything is known. (FC Ep VIII 16)

Our King has not abandoned us. He is with us and He has given us much to do. Read Matthew 5:13–14. Then read the following:

The dual calling of a Christian to faith and love means that we are not evacuated from the world, sucked up by a celestial vacuum cleaner into the safety of heaven. Like salt, believers are sprinkled through creation. Like light they are left in the world to penetrate its darkness. Faith receives God's gifts, and as these gifts have their way with us, they move us to give as the Lord has given all things to us. (p. 249)

What, then, is the tension in which God's people live? How do God's people live out their vocations in a sinful world that does not understand the Gospel or God's people?

Lifting it up

Heavenly Father, grant Your mercy and grace to Your people in their many and various callings. Give them patience, and strengthen them in their Christian vocation of witness to the world and of service to their neighbor in Christ's name; through Jesus Christ, our Lord. (194)

HYMN

I love Your kingdom, Lord,
The place of Your abode,
The Church our blest Redeemer saved
With His own precious blood.
—"I Love Your Kingdom, Lord" (LSB 651:1)

CHAPTERS 33 AND 34

We Tell Others and We Share Our Blessings

pp. 250–56

BELIEVE, TEACH, CONFESS

Our love for God, even though it is small, cannot possibly be separated from faith. For we come to the Father through Christ. When forgiveness of sins has been received, then we are truly certain that we have a God (Exodus 20:3), that is, that God cares for us. We call upon Him, we give Him thanks, we fear Him, we love Him as 1 John 4:9 teaches, "We love because He first loved us." In other words, we love Him because He gave His Son for us and forgave our sins. In this way John shows that faith comes first and love follows. (Ap V 20)

Key Bible Verse

So, being affectionately desirous of you, we were ready to share with you not only the gospel of God but also our own selves, because you had become very dear to us. (1 Thessalonians 2:8)

Review

1. We learn from God's large and gracious heart that the same gifts He gives to us are to be given and shared with others. We are to be generously joyful with the Good News of salvation through Jesus. Because of the Good News of Jesus we are to be joyfully generous with God's gifts to us.

Consider the Key Bible Verse above. How does Paul cover in the same passage both the topic of telling others and the topic of sharing with others?

Connect

2. Read Mark 2:15–17. In Chapter 20 we learned that Jesus ate dinner with sinners, and certainly still does in His Holy Supper. But was Jesus silent at such meals? Did Jesus just exude grace and forgiveness, so the sinners through the process of osmosis could soak them up? No. Jesus spoke. We learn in Luke 15:1, "Now the tax collectors and sinners were all drawing near to hear [Jesus]." How did Jesus bring people to Himself?

3. There is always conversation around food and drink. Read again pages 253–54. How then do we bring others to hear the holy conversation Jesus wants to have with sinners, sinners you might invite? Out of the twelve suggestions on page 254, do you think you could choose two to do?

4. The earthly gifts we share with others are as important as the gift of God's love shared with others. Read Exodus 31:17. What word surprises you the most in this passage?

5. Now read Romans 15:30–33; Philemon 7; and 2 Corinthians 7:13. What common theme do you find among these passages?

Ponder

6. Dig deep into the Scripture passages available from this past Sunday—the introit, the Psalm, the gradual, the Old Testament, Epistle and Gospel readings. How might you use the Scripture readings from this past Sunday to tell someone about Jesus? Were there any words of encouragement, hope, or strength to share with just one person? Even if you're not comfortable speaking such words to someone, do you know two people who could use a note of Gospel-centered encouragement?

7. God doesn't give you 90 percent of what you need and withhold 10 percent for Himself. God gives you everything you have and need. God doesn't need our gifts—but your neighbor does! What, then, does God give to you so that you can be challenged with all wisdom and good stewardship to give to others?

> **HYMN**
>
> We give Thee but
>   Thine own,
> Whate'er the gift may be;
> All that we have is Thine alone,
> A trust, O Lord, from Thee.
> The captive to release,
> To God the lost to bring,
> To teach the way of life and peace,
> It is a Christ-like thing.
> —"We Give Thee But Thine Own"
>   (*LSB* 781:1, 5)

Pray

Gracious Lord Jesus, You have given us Your precious Word, not to keep to ourselves, but to proclaim to many others. Give us the boldness to do so. Not only have You given us the rich gift of the Gospel, but so also do You give us everything we own and have. Help us to share Your many blessings entrusted to our care. In Your abundantly full and giving name we pray. Amen.

Putting It All Together pp. 257–61

Looking it up

The Formula of Concord, Solid Declaration, is the final document in the Book of Concord. The Solid Declaration was written and published in 1577. The collected documents in the Book of Concord were officially published as a whole in 1580. We read once again about Jesus:

> We unanimously believe, teach, and confess the following about the righteousness of faith before God, in accordance with the comprehensive summary of our faith and confession presented above. A poor sinful person is justified before God, that is, absolved and declared free and exempt from all his sins and from the sentence of well-deserved condemnation, and is adopted into sonship and inheritance of eternal life, without any merit or worth of his own. This happens without any preceding, present, or subsequent works, out of pure grace, because of the sole merit, complete obedience, bitter suffering, death, and resurrection of our Lord Christ alone. His obedience is credited to us for righteousness. (FC SD III 9)

In *Lutheranism 101* we read:

> Lutherans talk about the "chief article," "the doctrine upon which the Church rises and falls." That refers to the teaching of justification by faith, or to be more technical, justification by grace through faith in the work of Christ—in other words, the Gospel, the Good News of salvation through Christ.

> In Lutheran theology, everything goes back to this. (p. 261)

And that is where we close, with Jesus, who is "the Alpha and the Omega, the first and the last, the beginning and the end" (Revelation 22:13).

Linking it up

We now come full circle in our study. What began with God ends with God. At every turn of a page you now expect to hear about Jesus and how He has saved you from your sins. You are blessed to have learned so much from so many. List three things you didn't know that you now know or have come to know in a different or fuller way. Then list three things you need or want to study further.

1. _____

_____

_____

_____

2. _____

_____

_____

_____

1. _____

_____

_____

_____

2. _____

_____

_____

_____

3. _____

_____

_____

_____

3. _____

_____

_____

_____

Lifting it up

O Lord God, heavenly Father, You gave Your only Son to die for our sins and to rise again for our justification. By Your Holy Spirit grant us newness of life that through the power of Christ's resurrection we may dwell with Him forever; through the same Jesus Christ, our Lord. (184)

HYMN

Come, Thou Fount
    of ev'ry blessing,
Tune my heart to sing Thy grace;
Streams of mercy, never ceasing,
Call for songs of loudest praise.
While the hope of endless glory
Fills my heart with joy and love,
Teach me ever to adore Thee;
May I still Thy goodness prove.
Oh, that day when freed from
    sinning,
I shall see Thy lovely face;
Clothed then in the blood-washed
    linen,
How I'll sing Thy wondrous grace!
Come, my Lord, no longer tarry;
Take my ransom'd soul away;
Send Thine angels soon to carry
Me to realms of endless day.
—"Come, Thou Fount of Every
    Blessing" (*LSB* 686:1, 4)

A Pastor's Daily Prayer

O Almighty God, merciful Father, I, a poor, miserable sinner, confess unto Thee all my sins and iniquities; especially do I acknowledge my indolence in prayer, my neglect of Thy Word, and my seeking after good days and vainglory. But I am heartily sorry for them and sincerely repent of them; and I pray Thee, of Thy boundless mercy and for the sake of the holy, innocent, bitter sufferings and death of Thy beloved Son, forgive me all my sins, and be gracious and merciful to me. Yea, cleanse me through Thy Spirit by the blood of Jesus Christ, and give me more and more power and willingness to strive after holiness, for Thou hast called me that I should be holy and blameless before Thee in love.

I thank Thee also, O faithful God, for my family, my wife and children, and for all my relatives. Thou hast given them to me purely out of fatherly, divine goodness and mercy, without any merit or worthiness in me. Preserve them in good health, and give them their daily bread; but above all keep them in Thy grace and in the true confession of Thy name unto the end.

Thou, O God of all grace and mercy, hast also called me, a poor unworthy sinner, to be a servant of Thy Word and hast placed me into that office which preaches the reconciliation and hast given me this flock to feed. In and by myself I am wholly incompetent to perform the work of this great office; and, therefore, I pray Thee, make me an able minister of Thy Church. Give me Thy Holy Spirit, the Spirit of wisdom and knowledge, of grace and prayer, of power and strength, of courage and joyfulness, of sanctification and the fear of God. Fill me with the right knowledge, and open my lips that my mouth may proclaim the honor of Thy name. Fill my heart with a passion for souls and with skillfulness to give unto each and every sheep or lamb entrusted to my care what is due unto it at the proper time. Give me at all times sound advice and just works; and wherever I overlook something or in the weakness of my flesh speak or act wrongly, do Thou set it aright, and help that no one may through me suffer harm to his soul.

Glory and honor, praise and thanks be unto Thee, God, Father, Son, and Holy Ghost, for all the mercy and faithfulness Thou hast shown to this congregation. Thy Word has not returned unto Thee void, but Thou hast here gathered a people that knows Thee and fears Thy name. Give me Thy Holy Spirit, that I may at all times see the good things in this congregation and praise and thank Thee for them. Bless Thy Word in the future, that it may preserve the believers in Thy grace, convert those that are not yet Thine, and bring back the erring and delinquent. Gather Thy people as a hen gathereth her chickens under her wins, and be Thou a wall of fire round about Thy congregation.

Graciously take into Thy fatherly care the sick and the needy, all widows and orphans, and all who are in any trouble, temptation, anguish of labor, peril of death, or any other adversity. Comfort them, O God, with Thy Holy Spirit, that they may patiently endure their afflictions and acknowledge them as a manifestation of Thy fatherly will. Preserve their soul from faintheartedness and despondency, and help that they may seek Thee, the great Physician of their souls. And if any pass through the valley of the shadow of death, suffer them not, in the last hour, for any pain or fear of death, to fall away from Thee, but let Thine everlasting arms be underneath them, and grant them a peaceful departure and a happy entrance into Thine eternal kingdom.

Furthermore, I pray Thee, Thou wouldst at all times fill the offices of this congregation and its societies with upright, honest, and sincere men and women, who have the welfare of their congregation at heart and are able to help me in my office with their counsel and their deeds. Unite their hearts with me in love for the truth; give them the spirit of prayer for me and for their congregation, so that we may in unity and harmony build Thy kingdom in this place.

And since hypocrites and ungodly people are often found within the visible church organization, I pray Thee, do not permit Satan to disrupt this congregation through such or to hinder the efficiency of my office. If there are such in our midst, let Thy Word be like unto a hammer upon their hearts of stone. Have patience with them; but if they persist in their unbelief, hypocrisy, and wickedness, do Thou reveal them, so that they may be put forth from Thy congregation. Give me a forgiving heart towards all, and help me, especially for their sake, to speak and act cautiously.

Preserve and keep the youth of our Church from falling away and joining the world, and keep them from the many sins of youth. Thou, O Lord, knowest how difficult it is to lead the young on the right paths and to divide the Word of Truth with respect to them; do Thou, therefore, give me particular wisdom and skill to be stern without estranging their hearts, and mild and charitable without strengthening them in frivolity and unruliness.

Mercifully bless the education and instruction of the children, that they may grow up in Thy fear to the praise of Thy name. I commend unto Thee also the nursery of our church, the Christian day school. Hinder and frustrate all enemies of this institution. May I ever regard and accept it as a precious gift of God! Give our congregation able and apt teachers. Preserve them from an indecent and evil walk and conversation. Bless the work of our Sunday school teachers, and help them to lead the little ones into the Savior's loving arms.

To Thy grace and mercy I also commend all my brethren in office. Arrest and suppress all discord and dissension. Give me a brotherly heart towards all true humility, and help me to bear with patience their casual weakness or deficiencies. Grant that they also may act as true brethren toward me.

Keep and preserve our whole Synod, its teachers and officers, true to Thy Word. Cause the work of our Synod to grow. Guard and protect all members of Synod against sinful ambitions, dissension, and indifference in doctrine and practice. Bless all higher institutions of learning, our colleges, seminaries, and university. Accompany all missionaries on their dangerous ways, and help them to perform their work. Gather the elect from all nations into Thy holy Christian Church, and bring them at last into Thy Church Triumphant in heaven.

Grant also health and prosperity to all that are in authority in our country, especially to * the President and Congress of the United States, the Governor and Legislature of this State, and to all Judges and Magistrates.

* (His Majesty the King of the British Commonwealth of Nations, the Governor-General and the Prime Minister of our Dominion, as well as the Premier of our Province, and all Governments and Parliaments, and all Judges and Magistrates. [For Use in the British Empire])

Endue them with grace to rule after Thy good pleasure, to the maintenance of righteousness and to the hindrance and punishment of wickedness, that we may lead a quiet and peaceable life in all godliness and honesty.

Hear me, most merciful God, in these my humble requests, which I offer up unto Thee in the name of Jesus Christ, Thy Son, our Lord, to whom, with Thee and the Holy Ghost, be all honor and glory, world without end. Amen.

—From *The Lutheran Agenda* (St. Louis: Concordia, n.d.), 117–20.